BEYOND DEATH

BEYOND DEATH
LIFE IN THE HEREAFTER

FRANJO TERHART

p

Copyright © Parragon Books Ltd
Queen Street House
4 Queen Street
Bath BA1, 1 HE, UK

Original edition: ditter projektagentur GmbH
Project coordination and picture research:
  Inna Ditter-Hilkens
Editing: Ulrike Kraus
Series design: Claudio Martinez
Layout and typesetting: Maizkorn Kommuni-
  kation & Gestaltung, Gerd Turke

American edition produced by: APE Int'l
Translation: Russell Cennydd, Christine Yoshida

ISBN: 978-1-4054-8961-4

Printed in Malaysia

CONTENTS

**The Hereafter in
the Major Religions** 34

**Outside
Mainstream Religions** 54

**Modern Concepts
of the Afterlife** 70

BEYOND DEATH

Life as part of a greater whole

Quite early in human history, our ancestors already believed that earthly life was only one part of a greater whole. Early peoples thought of the hereafter as a terra incognita on the map of life, and colored in the empty spaces with pictures and ideas that varied depending on their local culture and religions.

In most peoples' beliefs, life continues beyond the last breath and into another world—a world which often isn't all that different from the one left behind.

Belief in the hereafter began in the Stone Age

The belief in a life after death probably reaches back to the Stone Age. Although people already had language at that time, they were not able to document their thoughts. They did, however, decorate the walls of their caves with mysterious symbols, such as spirals, circles, and points. According to research, they presumably wanted to express that life consists of more than just hunting and the daily fight for survival. From the very beginning, humankind seems to have believed

that death was not a final end to existence, but merely a border crossing. The idea that earthly life couldn't be all there was to experience was shared by the Siberian shaman as well as the Aztec and Inca peoples of South America, the Celts and Teutonic tribes in northwestern Europe, and the various native tribes of Africa. All of them developed concepts of life after death that are similar in some ways, but differ in others.

Burial gifts for a new life

Burial gifts are evidence of the belief in a life after death or, alternatively, in a journey to another world. Even Neanderthals placed flowers in the graves of their dead.

Over time, ideas about a life after death became more differentiated. The supposition of some cultures that the body has an immortal soul whose appearance wasn't terribly different from the physical body was quite common. The deceased found themselves reincarnated in their ethereal bodies in a hereafter that reflected their previous cultural backgrounds and religious worlds. Deceased Native Americans of the Plains region experienced a lovely prairie world in the kingdom of the dead, while the Egyptians relived their social life. What they had in common was ample food and continuing peace for all of eternity. The conviction that everything is better on "the other side" is a firm part of the concept of the hereafter.

Exploration of the realms of the afterlife

The following chapters will be an expedition—a journey of a special kind into the realm of the afterlife according to a variety of cultures and religions. It

Burial gifts testify to belief in a life after death or, alternatively, in a journey to another world. The higher the social rank of the deceased, the more precious the burial gifts offered.

People will always ask the question "Is there life after death?" Cemeteries are not only places of mourning and remembrance of the dead, but also are gateways between the here and the hereafter.

wouldn't be accurate to say that early humans simply invented the hereafter. The belief in a world after earthly death goes beyond the conceptions of religion and local culture, highlighting many of the essential expectations and hopes of all humankind.

The Iranian poet and mathematician Omar Khayyam (approximately 1048–1122) brought it to the point when he wrote, "I sent my soul through the invisible, some letter of that afterlife to spell; and by and by my soul returned to me, and answered, 'I myself am Heav'n and Hell'." (*The Rubaiyat*, FitzGerald's translation)

In other words, what we experience in the hereafter is exactly what we expect and believe it to be during our lifetime.

Nowadays, people occasionally relate so-called "near-death experiences" after they have been brought back to the world of the living through the skills of modern medicine. In a manner not very different from that of the adepts of Greek mystery cults, they explain that dying is an inauguration or initiation into a new life. The experiences reported by people who have been at the threshold of life and death largely reflect their respective expectations.

Visionaries such as Emanuel Swedenborg or Princess Eugenie von der Leyen were visited by the spirits of the departed. Their descriptions of the hereafter reflect Christian ideas of purgatory and punishment.

A topography of the hereafter, worldwide and in all times

It has always been important for people of all cultures and times to have as clear a picture of the hereafter as possible, whether they were Egyptians, Greeks, ingidenous peoples or advanced religions, occultists, spiritualists or mystics.

This phenomenon spans the globe, once again showing how intensively the respective religions and specific cultural characteristics imprint various understandings of the hereafter. Although many motifs are similar and frequently reoccur, quite a variety of concepts have arisen. On the following pages, images of the afterlife drawn from the viewpoints of different peoples, religions, and media of all eras and cultures will be presented and explored. All of them together

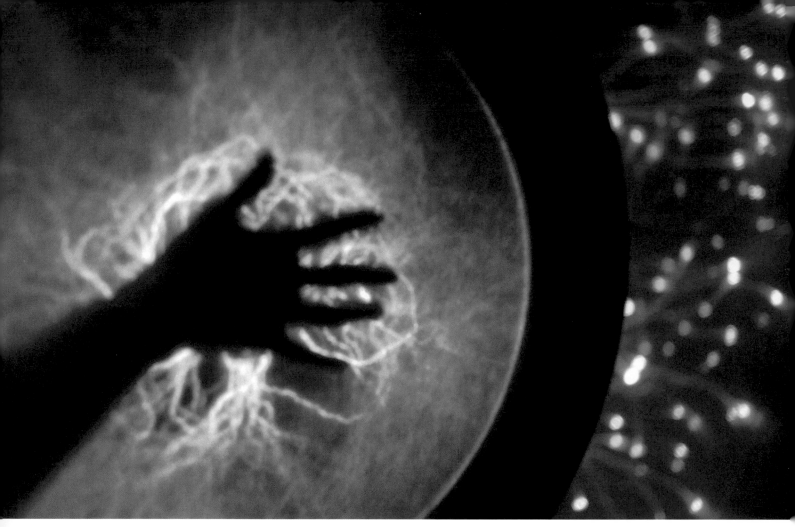

Mediums claim they can see auras, for example those of a hand. They see colors of different intensities that indicate illnesses as well as one's state of mind.

contribute to the design of a thrilling topography, a one-of-a-kind map of the hereafter.

The multifaceted human body

According to the beliefs of many ancient peoples and religions, three immaterial or subtle bodies (the etheric, astral, and mental bodies)—in addition to the physical body—play an important role in our living and dying.

All four together create the complete human being, giving the person a place in the secular as well as spiritual worlds. This conception of humans, consisting of a physically mortal and yet at the same time immaterial and immortal body, appears in different variations time and again in human ideas about the mystery of death. In general one can differentiate between the following concepts.

The aura

First of all, people are said to have an aura, which can be perceived by spiritually gifted people. It surrounds the body as life energy. Numerous people have studied and written about the aura, for example Theophrastus Paracelsus (1494–1541) in the Middle Ages, the Austrian doctor Franz Anton Mesmer (1734–1815) who introduced the concept of "animal magnetism," also known as mesmerism, and London physician Walter Kilner (1847–1920), who strove to make the aura visible using technical means.

The Russian Semyon Davidovich Kirlian introduced the most recent technical procedure in 1939. He had discovered a photographic technique known today as Kirlian photography. Using this technique, the corona radiance is made visible on exposed material, making it possible to study the auras of living beings.

The three subtle bodies

In esoteric and other spiritual doctrines, one usually refers to two or three subtle bodies in addition to the physical body. This system corresponds to those of some ancient peoples (for example, the Egyptians) and different religious faiths (e.g. Hinduism). The following is an introduction, giving a description of these other human "bodies" which normally cannot be perceived by the naked eye.

1. The etheric body is responsible for sustaining the physical processes. It functions as a kind of barometer of personal well-being. There are healers who are able to diagnose illnesses through analysis of the etheric body alone. When the physical body dies, the etheric body also dies.

2. The astral body processes feelings. It is formed from all the wishes, emotions, and thoughts that are contained in the human mind. This subtle body is the vehicle for astral projections or other out-of-body experiences. Upon physical death, it leaves the body and enters the astral world. It can also spontaneously leave the physical body due to accidents, comas, or the influence of drugs. The astral body is that part of us that is abroad during near-death experiences and shares the details of them later.

3. The mental body is the repository of all our thoughts, including extrasensory and intuitive perceptions. People in deep meditative states are able to recognize their higher self and have spiritual experiences through this body.

On the other hand, the mental body is completely connected to the earthly and material world, which is not to be taken negatively. In Tibetan Buddhism, the mental body allows an adept to see through the illusion of the world—which Buddhists don't consider to be real—and reach true awareness.

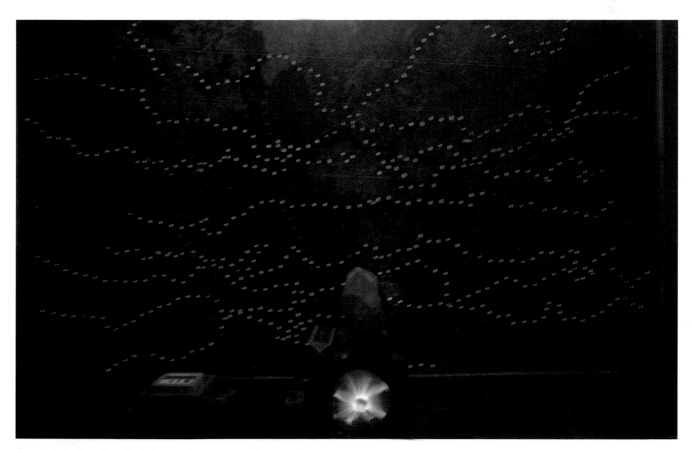

The subtle body is the vehicle for astral projections. Upon death, it is released from the body forever and enters the astral world. During near-death experiences, the astral body can travel through walls.

ANCIENT PEOPLE'S BELIEFS
IN THE AFTERLIFE

EGYPT

A strange custom

The Greek writer Herodotus (485 BC–ca. 425 BC) told of an unusual Egyptian custom he observed during his visit to the Land of the Pharaohs in 460 BC. Herodotus wrote that at every banquet, the Egyptians would circle the guests with a corpse in a vessel—what is meant is a small, mummy-like figure—to remind them of their mortality.

Herodotus immediately provided an explanation for this behavior, which seems quite peculiar from our modern perspective. The Egyptians explained the custom to him as follows: "Look at this vessel carefully, then drink and amuse yourself! For when you are dead, you will look just the same." (1) The motivation behind this behavior wasn't mourning for the dead person, but rather, in accordance with Egyptian beliefs, an invitation from the little mummy to enjoy life.

Thoughts on eternity

The ancient Egyptians apparently had a distinct awareness of the temporal limits of earthly life. The unavoidable presence of death was the reason they tried to stop time through their deeds and faith. The impulse to immortalize themselves is highly apparent in ancient Egyptian art, the great pyramids, and Egyptian mummies. The Egyptians wanted to leave something everlasting for eternity. Egyptian pictures frequently indicate the eternal, as does the cult of mummification. Ancient Egypt will always be associated with its innumerable mummies, which leads to the question: for what purpose were the dead bodies so elaborately bandaged and buried?

The meaning of mummification

The first step toward mummification was to remove the internal organs and brain. These were placed in special jars to be stored in the burial chamber later on. The

In order to stop the passage of time with their deeds and faith, the ancient Egyptian people of the Nile built "pyramids for eternity." Even the Egyptians' images almost always referred to the eternal.

Mummies like this one are evidence of the ancient Egyptians' strong desire to preserves themselves for eternity. Mummified, the dead remained intact. Burial gifts were offered in order to feed, dress, and adorn the deceased.

The two parts of the soul—Ba and Ka

Ba means something along the lines of soul, or personality, while Ka is that part of the soul that contains the life force. The Ka was able to live longer through the process of mummification.

Ka is something impersonal, while Ba means the individual, the personality or soul itself. At the time of death, the Ba separates itself from the body and usually dissolved completely in the kingdom of the dead, if the "self" had not become aware and competent during life. For initiates of the mysteries however, the Ba lived on as the true "Self," because the adept was conscious of the spiritual world prior to physical death.

body was conserved through mummification. In this way, the deceased would remain whole. Although the flesh shrank, the deceased retained his body, lived in a "house"—the burial chamber—and was fed, dressed, and adorned by means of the burial offerings. The Egyptians created a kind of "living" corpse which needed to be provided for. In Egyptian belief, the deceased resided not only in the burial chamber, but in heaven and the kingdom of the dead as well. While heaven was at first reserved for deceased royalty, later it could also be claimed by their subjects.

A series of sarcophagus texts illustrates the heavenly existence of the deceased. An ancient Egyptian arrives in the kingdom of the dead, where the Ba, his bird-shaped and man-headed soul, connects with heaven. Mummification of the body is a prerequisite for ascension into heaven, since the Ba must return to the body every night.

Osiris, ruler of the dead

According to Egyptian mythology, Osiris, the husband and brother of Isis, was murdered and carved up by his brother Set, who wanted to be sole ruler over the people. However, Isis succeeded in putting her beloved together again, enabling Osiris to rise up from the dead. Through Osiris, Isis gave birth to Horus, the

The god Osiris is the supreme judge in the court of the dead (on the left, standing between two women).

falcon god of the sky, to be Osiris' heir and avenger. During a tribunal of the gods, it was decided that Osiris should rule over the underworld and its countless dead. In this way, Osiris became the supreme judge of the deceased. Resurrection would be possible for anyone if they had dedicated himself to the mysteries of the god during life. To do so, they must symbolically imitate the death of Osiris. Only through experiencing this initiation could life continue and endure in the hereafter.

The Egyptian sky is female

The sky was female in the faith of the ancient Egyptians. Nut was the goddess of the sky and mother of Osiris. She said "I will give birth to you anew, into rejuvenation." (2) All who had not been "reborn" by Nut were condemned to dwindle away in the kingdom of the dead; they were to literally "rot in hell." The

mystery initiates needed to work their way through the hereafter with its myriad gates and halls. Demonic creatures populated every chamber and posed a great danger for the soul on its journey. The deceased moved through the underworld by means of their voices: calling, conjuring, intimidating, pleading, answering, or threatening. Their knowledge about important names, gods, and rites of the cult protected them from the demons and helped them along their path to Osiris.

The Book of Amduat

The journey through the underworld was fraught with danger. Demonic gatekeepers continuously threatened the deceased, trying to catch them in nets. Moreover, the deceased needed to show that they deserved to live as the gods in the hereafter. The path of the soul desiring to find Osiris, ultimately becoming "like the great god himself," is described in several funerary books. The oldest of these is the Book of Amduat (*Amduat* literally means "that which is in the afterworld").

One area of Osiris' kingdom of the dead can be called heavenly. But a second side of it existed as well, which was heinous and appalling. There was a dearth of everything in this awful domain: water, bread, and light. Horrible, demonic creatures created bloodbaths by cutting off heads, slicing through throats, and ripping hearts out of chests. Deep horror drove the deceased to try and escape from this realm "where the stars fall from the sky onto their faces, not knowing how to raise themselves up again." (2) Humans had to eat their own excrement; everything was transformed to its opposite.

The dead who did not know what was expected of them were damned to this hellish realm for eternity. Those who had been previously initiated, however, and had the necessary knowledge, were able to successfully negotiate the twenty-one gates, seven halls and fifteen cities of the underworld. Only then could they take their place in Osiris' realm as equals to the other gods. Through this ordeal the initiate experienced the "journey of the sun through the night," passing many tests while traveling through the underworld.

One hundred and ninety spells as a guide through the hereafter

The celebrated Book of Amduat showed Egyptians who followed the path of the mysteries how to overcome death. The initiates learned all the essential information through its 190 spells, or teachings. Everything was rehearsed in the hope that the knowledge and accomplishments learned during life would be effective in the actual situation of death.

Describing the journey of a pharaoh through the underworld after his death, the book's aim was for the dead to be united with the realm of "perpetual duration." The dead man whose journey is described says, "I am the Ba (the soul) of Osiris and with him am reunited." (2) The mystery initiate repels the darkness of the netherworld, becoming "rejuvenated, renewed, and restored." He becomes an "Osiris, lord of eternity." The experience took place through an initiation rite, enabling him to go through life and death as one of the "awoken." According to the mystery cult beliefs, the awoken one entered the tail of a snake, exiting through its mouth as a rejuvenated young man. However, one of the final tests before the dead could take the final step into the hereafter was the Court of Death.

Osiris was the lord of the underworld and of the dead. He was killed, only to be resurrected from the dead. Those who believed in him would likewise rise again.

Nut, the ancient Egyptian's sky goddess and Osiris' mother, said "I will give birth to you anew, into rejuvenation." (2) But only those initiated into the mysteries experienced this rebirth—all others were left to rot.

The court of death with forty-two judges

The Court of Death was found in the "Hall of Two Truths" under the auspices of Osiris. Living one's life in a proper and pure way was mandatory in order to abide in the hereafter. The deceased was required to know Osiris' name to even consider taking the next step. Accordingly, he was first asked for the name of the lord of the realm: "Who is this?"—"Osiris"—"Then come forward Soul, you have been registered."

Only at this point was the soul allowed to be presented before the court, where the deceased was initially asked four questions. "Why have you come?"—"To be registered."—"What are your qualifications?"—"I am free of any and all sin."—"To whom should I register you?"—"To him whose house has ceilings of fire, whose walls are of living Uraei (falcon-winged cobras) and whose floors are the deluge." All of this was intended to describe the realm of Osiris.

There were forty-two judges in Osiris' realm of the dead. Before them the deceased had to recite the forty-two sins and swear he had committed none of them.

The Negative Confessions

Now the deceased had to list for the gods of judgment the forty-two sins, or principles of Ma'at, and declare the purity of his soul by assuring the judges that he had committed none of them. In this way he held true to the ritual formula of the "Negative Confessions." He was interrogated using the formula "Thou shall not…" followed by specific offences such as betrayal, boasting, deception, embezzlement, adultery, and theft. The deceased answered saying, "I have not…" filling in the blank with the appropriate sin. The forty-two judges then weighed every answer.

Weighed and found too heavy?

While the deceased declared the purity of his soul, his heart, thought to be the essence of human nature, was weighed by the jackal god Anubis in comparison to the

The game of senet

The Egyptians knew a board game called "senet," which means something like "passing by" or "happening." Senet was played by two people on a playing board with three rows of ten squares. Some of the squares were marked with numbers, some with the symbols for heaven and hell, and others contained symbols for people or the gods. The point of the game was to pass through all thirty squares with their different messages of blessing or damnation, weaving a path over the board in order to be the first to collect all of the opponent's pieces. This game, documented in funerary texts and burial finds, was often played simply for fun. It also had a religious meaning, however, and was used to simulate the transition of the soul into the eternal afterlife. Illustrated in the tomb of the priest Sennedjem, the game's goal is access to and acquisition of eternal sustenance.

weight of the feather of Ma'at, goddess of truth and justice. This feather represented truth and order in the world. The scribe god Thoth recorded the results. If the deceased's heart was found to be heavier than the feather, that signified the soul was laden with guilt and unable to be saved. The heart was then eaten by Ammut, devourer of the dead, in a dark and gloomy valley, leaving the soul to die again a second and final time.

Heavenly society

If declared free of all sin, the deceased was allowed to live in the hereafter and accepted as a member of the heavenly society. There he received food, drink and a house. The Egyptian concept of life in the hereafter and of the society of the blessed drew from the example of life on this side of the underworld.

Those souls declared innocent were believed to have unlimited access to the food of the gods, as well as a right to eternal life in the netherworld. There was nothing more an Egyptian could hope to receive for having lived a virtuous life.

The god Thoth was the Egyptian lord of magic. Writing on a papyrus roll, now in the Cairo Museum, says that he who invokes the first spell of Thoth will be able to understand the language of the animals.

This painting by Michelangelo shows Charon ferrying the dead across the River Styx to Hades. The Greek underworld was a place without hope of return, full of shadows and fear.

GREECE AND ROME

Mystery initiation as a shield against the desolate underworld

"I came to the border crossing between life and death. I crossed over into the underworld at the threshold of Proserpina (queen of the dead) and after traveling through all four elements I returned again." (3)

This text was written over two thousand years ago by an unnamed member of an ancient mystery cult. *Mysterium* translates as meaning something intended only for initiates, the so-called *mystai*, thus only for a very exclusive circle of people. The people of classical antiquity believed that through initiation into the mysteries they would have access to the power of the gods and would be granted a life after death. Those who hadn't been inducted were destined for the underworld of Hades.

What the mystai experienced during the initiation was a symbolic or ritual experience of death. Darkness, entrapment, and complete isolation were elements of the ritual, all skillfully staged by priests of the cult. For the believers this was no staged theatrical act, but rather their salvation at the time of their actual death. They would be able to continue on in the hereafter as their true "self," and not merely as a shadow.

Different mystery cults

Various mystery cults developed in antiquity, such as the Eleusinian Mysteries in Greece or the Mysteries of Mithras toward the end of the Roman Empire. The purpose of initiation into a mystery cult was to attain secret knowledge unknown to those outside the cult; of course one had to remain silent about this information. With this knowledge, the mystery initiates were able to more deeply perceive the divine and the human, the earthly and the celestial. Moreover, initiates were able to relinquish once and for all their fear of death and the horror of Hades. An initiate had an easier path through the hereafter than the one that lay ahead of most people.

The gods become human

The initiation occurred primarily through drawing connections between the individual's life and those of the gods. People identified with the gods when they saw the deities experiencing feelings similar to their own, for example, when Demeter mourned the abduction of her daughter, Persephone, by Hades, the god of the underworld. This created a bond between the gods and humans, a connection so strong that the people of antiquity knew they would be together with their gods even after death. The initiated felt that they were related to the gods through grief, pain, and fear. What may seem insignificant today was actually a radical change in the ancient religious world. Previously, the gods had been regarded as superior beings far removed from the earthly sphere. One

The remains of a Roman temple dedicated to Mithras show the god with his favorite animal, the bull. Mithras was honored as a sun god who fought the forces of darkness. Wild bulls were sacrificed to him.

could pray to them and beg for their support, but it was a completely new idea that they, too, mourned as people do and that they suffered. That is what made them similar to people. But only initiates of the mystery cults experienced this human-like behavior of the deities.

The horrible realm of the lord of the dead

A different fate awaited those who had not been initiated in the mysteries: a hereafter cold and dead, full of horrors and danger. The god Hades ruled the underworld together with his wife, Persephone (whom he had abducted; they were later known in Roman mythology as Pluto and Proserpine). After death, one landed forever in their cold and dark world, which was called the "Realm of Shadows" for good reason. A shadow is not alive; it is feeble and weak. A shadow has no individuality. To the ancient Greeks and Romans, to be dead meant to lead just such a shadow existence for all of eternity. That was the main reason why the people of antiquity tried to enjoy themselves as much as possible during life.

According to myth, Demeter's daughter Persephone was abducted by Hades, god of the underworld. Demeter's grief over her child consoled people, showing that gods experienced the same emotions they did.

Mysteries and initiation as an alternative

Mystery cults arose over the course of time, and they spread from Asia Minor and Egypt into Europe. The mysteries stood in contrast to the traditional worship of the divine through their deep piety to their cult, the colorfulness of their exotic rites, and their fascination with secrecy. They also gave a new identity to their initiates. "Initiation," they promised, "allows you to survive death with your character and personality intact. Those who have not been initiated must wallow in mud, carrying water in a sieve for all of eternity." It was also written that "the uninitiated are filtered out, only to be destroyed by the guardians of the gates." (3)

Experiencing god through ecstasy

All that we know about the actual sequence of events of the mystery rituals is information divulged by those who participated, but in the end no longer wanted to

Demeter, goddess of fertility and the harvest, was honored as Mother Earth. Through her daughter, Persephone, she was also associated with the gloomy, cold realm of the dead.

The entrance to the underworld was marked by the waters of horror of the River Styx. Passage over the Styx was made possible by the ferryman Charon, who brought souls over the river into the underworld.

keep silent. An induction into a mystery cult must have been a unique and penetrating experience for every initiate. It is thought that certain ecstasy-inducing techniques were used to bring the initiates into a psychological state unlike anything they had ever experienced. Ecstasy enabled the initiates to perceive the supernatural. They might, for example, have a face-to-face meeting with the fertility goddesses Demeter (the "earth mother") or Cybele, "mother of the gods." Initiates perceived these experiences as absolutely real.

The introduction to the earth mother Demeter was experienced as follows: the initiate said with absolute conviction, "I am ash, ash is earth, the earth is a goddess, therefore I am not dead." (3) In this moment the initiate sensed a blissful connection with the goddess. He continued, "I have been received into the lap of the earth goddess." The initiate understood that a new life would spring from the lap of the goddess because life

and death are contained in each other. Without one there cannot be the other. Every initiate who participated in this rite was freed of all fear of death.

Cybele initiation and the rite of castration

In the Mysteries of Cybele, many men castrated themselves during the initiation rites out of pure bliss, sacrificing their fertility to the Great Mother and moving one step closer to priesthood within the cult. Each initiate knew himself to be unique in a circle of like-minded people, celebrating orgiastic ceremonies that included shrill flute playing, tambourines, castanets, and ecstatic dancing. Conviction and the community gave the initiate strength and the assuredness that they had escaped death forever.

Acheron, Styx, and the ferryman Charon

Without an initiation into the mysteries, an insignificant existence awaited everyone in the underworld's realm of the dead, whether they be a proud king, a brave hero, or a famous commander. According to Greek mythology, the entrance to the underworld was marked by the River Acheron, where currents of fire and lament joined with the River Styx and its waters of horror. The ferryman Charon was responsible for bringing the dead across these rivers in his boat. This crossing is described in the Odyssey, the famous epic poem written by Homer.

On the shores of the realm of the dead, the three-headed dog Cerberus (also recorded as having fifty or one hundred heads) guarded the gate through which the deceased finally entered, never to return. Those who did not pay a coin to the ferryman for their crossing were thrown into the waters of horror. No one could escape from the life of shadows. There was no retribution in Hades, however. No one separated the sinners from the just. All of them spent their timeless existence in a musty, joyless, and relentlessly dark and gloomy realm.

The gods found Sisyphus to be too arrogant. As punishment, they decreed he would perpetually roll a boulder up a mountain, only to have it roll back down the slope again once he reaches the top.

The Elysian Fields

Even in contemporary time, however, there was a counterbalance to the mysteries and their horrifying vision of the underworld. In the fourth book of Homer's *Odyssey*, the gods escort the dying king Menalos to the edge of the world, where a pleasant life awaited him: there they found the famed Elysian Fields. The poet described them as a place "…where life is easiest for men. No snow is there, nor yet great storm, nor any rain…" (4) One could even say it was a paradise, a fertile land under an eternally clear blue sky, a realm of the gods. There one could not die, as death did not exist. The soul, however, was not separated from the body. That is why, as we learn from Homer, King Menalos continued to have feelings and could take pleasure in his surroundings. While the realm of shadows destroyed all life energy, there at the edge of the world was a land where one could lead an eternal life as a mortal.

Ambrosia and nectar as food of the eternal

The beautiful fields were a truly wonderful realm of salvation, with a guarantee that one would never die. One could also call it blessed because the people in Elysium were allowed to nourish themselves just as the gods did. Ambrosia and nectar were their food and drink, which according to the Greeks' beliefs gave the gods immortality. Elysium, the Elysian Fields (or Plains), or the Land of the Blessed are all names for this paradise beyond death. Elysium, however, should not be confused with the hereafter. Only the gods could decide who was allowed to stay there; no mortal could gain entrance against the gods' will.

Baptism of blood and resurrection

The members of the Cybele cult had to undergo a baptism of blood. During this initiation ritual, the *myste* (initiate) climbed into an earthen pit covered with planks. A bull was then slaughtered (ritually sacrificed) above the pit. The blood flowing down covered the initiates, who were also required to drink of the blood. In this way, the *myste* were supposed to experience death and resurrection.

In this respect, Christianity was able to supersede the mystery cults several centuries later. Here, too, was a god who suffered and mourned. Jesus even died for the people and rose again from the dead. In addition, the deceased maintained their full individuality. That was absolutely new in comparison with the previous mystery cults.

Tartarus, the dark abyss

But even for the apparently immortal, there was a "hell" into which they could be thrown, never to escape. Zeus, the supreme god of the Greeks, created a place of punishment in the darkest depths of the earth "that lies as deep in the earth as the sky stands over it." (3)

Zeus was the most powerful of the Greek gods. He sat enthroned on Mount Olympus and enjoyed interfering in the lives of mortals. Taking on different forms, he particularly loved to ensnare young girls.

This realm was called Tartarus or Tartaros. Tartarus was at the same time the deepest part of Hades. A powerful river of fire surrounded it like a belt, in addition to infinitely high steel walls. It was a place of no return that no mortal would ever wish to enter. When the Romans were threatened by the Huns in the fourth century AD, they called the invaders Tartars because it seemed as if their enemies came straight out of the fires of hell. Tartarus was by far the most horrible place one could imagine. Zeus banished the Titans to remain there, as well as Tantalus and Sisyphus and all those whom he deemed to be sinners and delinquents. Those who had to eke out their eternal lives in Tartarus couldn't sink any lower; they had become a no-thing. In comparison, the shadowy figures in the realm of Hades practically lived in a house of pleasure.

Homer wrote the *Iliad* and the *Odyssey*. The first epic poem describes the Trojan War; the second describes the wanderings of the hero Odysseus as he makes his way back home after the victorious war.

The deserted city of Machu Picchu in Peru is impressive taken as a whole. Streets and houses show that the standard of living must have been quite high. The Incas also believed in immortality of the soul.

INDIGENOUS PEOPLES

Belief in the soul

Almost all indigenous peoples came to believe in a soul that continues to exist after physical death. Settled in Central America, the Mayas believed that the deceased had to pass several hurdles such as dangerous rapids and deep canyons during their passage into the kingdom of the dead. The Incas in Peru developed similar ideas, including river crossings. On the other hand, the question of the whereabouts of the soul was answered by the different peoples in diverse ways.

The Aztecs' three realms of the dead

The Aztecs, who populated Mexico prior to the Spanish conquest, believed there were three different realms of the dead. People who died of illness, regardless of their social status, undertook an arduous journey to a region called Mictlan, where they perished. They died only after arriving in the hereafter, and were then permanently abolished. On the other hand, victims of natural disasters could expect paradisiacal conditions in the Tlalocan. The third group—those who died in battle and women who died in childbirth—were allowed into the "house of the sun," as the Aztecs

Happy hunting grounds

The Delaware Indians believed that everyone who had led a good life would live forever in paradise-like surroundings after death. This bountiful land was understood to be an island of exceptional beauty and great dimensions.

"A high mountain rises majestically from the center, and on the pinnacle is the home of the Great Spirit. The noblest of animals graze peacefully in uncountable herds and flocks over these laughing, beautiful, luxuriant plains.

Here the soul lives forever in a truly happy hunting ground. There children are reunited with their parents, and parents with their children. There is no sun, but rather a bright light which the creator allows to shine. All the people will look the same, and the blind and crippled will be completely healed."(5)

Ancestor veneration in Africa

The honoring of ancestors is of great importance in Africa. This is due to their firm conviction that an inseparable bond exists between the living and the dead. The prosperity and fruitfulness of a tribe depends on the well-being of their forebears. Therefore, the eldest members of the family receive special honor, as they are the closest to the ancestors in the hereafter. Rituals forge a connection between this world and the next. For traditional Africans, communion with their ancestors is of greater importance than closeness to God. They see no boundary between this world and the hereafter. Some tribes, for example, the Zulus, grant the dead higher status than the living.

The altered consciousness of the shaman

The altered awareness of shamans, the traditional healers of indigenous peoples, is described as an ecstatic trance. The shaman begins with drumming, chanting, dancing, jumping, and calls to the spirits, which often continue for several hours. At the peak of the trance, sometimes lying rigid and motionless on the ground, the shaman begins a spirit journey. At this point the spirit, independent of the physical body, travels into another world, whereby the soulless body, which was left behind, becomes the host of a guardian spirit. This exchange makes it possible for sickness to be healed and messages from the hereafter to be relayed as soon as the shaman has returned from the other world. Due to the long history of the Celtic migration out of the deepest reaches of Central Asia, there are historical and cultural connections between the shamanistic and Celtic otherworlds.

Sometimes we get a glimpse of the beauty of paradise here on earth. There are places in the world where nature's beauty is almost overwhelming. At the same time we associate nature with peace and happiness.

called it. The dead might have a human form, or they could also appear to the living as birds, clouds or the wind.

The two soul halves of the Ewe

The Ewe, a people consisting of various tribes living in the West African rainforest, believe in the preexistence or prenatal life of the soul in a spirit world identical to the earthly world. The birth of a child is at the same time the reincarnation of an ancestor. The soul then consists of two halves. The larger part—the life soul—comes from the spirit world or realm of the gods. The other, smaller half, in contrast—the death soul—comes from the underworld.

The life soul always returns to the divine spirit world, while the death soul begins a journey into the underworld. It is here, a place often referred to as the "house behind the river" that the death soul meets its ancestors. Provisions are necessary for this difficult and exhausting journey, which are provided through plentiful burial gifts. In contrast to the myths and beliefs of many other peoples and religions, famine is possible in the hereafter of the Ewe. During a famine, the soul can request food from the living. The food is then placed on the ground as a sacrificial offering.

THE CELTS

Celtic beliefs opposed to the Roman worldview

It is difficult to understand the Celts from today's point of view. This is due largely to the fact that their understanding of the world was so different from the modern view of things. The Celts originated from the area around the Caspian See in southern Russia before they spread throughout large parts of Western Europe sometime around the sixth century BC. Today, the remains of Celtic culture can be found primarily in Brittany, Wales, and Ireland. The Romans tried to destroy the Celts, among other reasons because their way of thinking was so strange to them. The Celtic belief that life didn't end after death didn't fit into the Roman conception of the world. Roman writers reported with horror how some Celts threw themselves of their own free will onto the funeral pyres of their relatives in order to share their new life in the hereafter with them. For a Roman, such behavior would have been incomprehensible.

Life and hereafter are two sides of the same coin

For the Celts, not only life and death belonged together like two sides of a coin; this was true of all contrasting elements in the world: good and evil as well as love and hate or war and peace.

In the Celtic worldview, life and the hereafter were expressions of one single world, which was at the same time visible and invisible. Death was therefore one part of the eternal circle of becoming and passing on. Fear of death was unnecessary because the soul was immortal. In this respect, a Celt could view death as the middle point of a long life, whereby the "middle point" was regarded as a transition or crossover.

From this perspective, life appeared to be endless. There was no beginning and no end, just an eternal continuation.

Druid wisdom

The white-clad druids with their characteristic long beards were the wise men or priests of the Celts. According to Pliny the elder (ca. 23–79 AD) the oak

In Ireland, Christian missionaries were received by the Celts with open arms. No Christian had to fear for their life here, partly due to the fact that the Celts skillfully melded their religion with that of the Christians.

The mistletoe was sacred to the druids because they hoped it would give them magical powers. Mistletoe could only be harvested with a golden sickle. The evergreen mistletoe was a symbol for eternal life.

Stonehenge was the center of the megalithic culture in the British Isles. The druids, clad in white, marked the change of season with secret rituals of life and death between Stonehenge's mighty sandstone blocks.

was their favorite tree, from which they cut mistletoe using a golden sickle at certain times of the year. They believed that mistletoe had magical powers. The druids knew about many medicinal plants and were skilled fortune tellers. Moreover, observations of nature made them good astronomers and skillful mathematicians.

According to their beliefs, the course of life and also individuals could be influenced by the spoken word—through incantations, curses, and magic spells. We have no written records from them, even though it is known that the majority of druids were capable of writing. Furthermore, they preferred to teach their hand-selected pupils in the forest because they were convinced that the essentials of life could be learned from trees. Their entire wisdom was passed on solely by word of mouth.

Bliss in the otherworld

Without doubt, the only traditional lore of the druids that was intended for the general populace was that of the immortality of the soul and its eternal life in the "otherworld." The otherworld was the Celtic hereafter, imagined as a paradisiacal place where food was available in overabundance. In addition, studying the Irish sagas of the Celtic gods and heroes that were collected by the monasteries on the island during the early Middle Ages lets us conclude that the immortal soul and so-called spirit journeys belonged to different aspects of the otherworld. The normal progress of the soul was immortality and crossing over into the otherworld, the Celtic land of utmost bliss.

The Celts believed that crossings into the realm of the dead could be found mainly near isolated lakes. The barriers between the here and the hereafter could fall, especially on the night of October 31st.

Spirit journey as the exception to the rule

The destiny to reach the otherworld was granted to all people—at least almost all. In contrast, the spirit journey was a fate reserved for certain legendary individuals. Some modern Celtic researchers believe, however, that it might have been possible under certain circumstances for a normal person to have been reincarnated as an animal. A few Celtic stories tell of such occurrences.

Crossovers into the kingdom of the dead

Death was nothing exceptional for the Celts, not even an important interruption of their lives. The invisible borders between the living and the dead were open once a year during Samhain, celebrated nowadays on the 31st of October.

According to Celtic beliefs, the otherworld or the land of the dead was not a specific place found under the ground or in the clouds. The dead were always near by the living and the living always near the dead. They lived, so to speak, next door to each other. The veil visually separating the two worlds would fall during Samhain, allowing this world and the other-world to meet without hindrance. It was as if a literal wall that separated the two realms disappeared.

The stories and chronicles of the Celtic culture often tell of mortals meeting and falling in love with

Excerpts from "The Voyages of Bran" (6)
'There is a distant isle,
Around which sea-horses glisten'
'Unknown is wailing or treachery
There is nothing rough or harsh,
But sweet music striking on the ear'
'It is a day of lasting weather
That showers silver on the lands'
Men and gentle women under a bush,
Without sin, without crime'
'We are from the beginning of creation
Without old age, without consummation of earth'

immortals, or of the living being carried off into the otherworld. Gods and people had a very natural and intimate contact with each other.

The beautiful image of the Celtic hereafter

Although the entranceway between the here and the otherworld was only open to ordinary mortals on Samhain, the gate was always left ajar for soothsayers and poets. The preferred crossings or portals into the realm of immortality were deep, dark forest lakes covered with a veil of mist or, most of all, the pre-historic megalith monuments. Mortals who arrived in the otherworld through those portals experienced something wondrous: the otherworld was like the real world down to the last detail. Here, too, there was an upper class that dressed themselves in exquisite gowns, whiling away the time with music and dance, continuous celebrations and delicious food and drink. Illness, worry, tears and death were unknown.

Even the weather was consistently mild. Although some old Irish texts refer to elves, monsters, apparitions, terrible ghosts and cruel witches who created mischief in this world of peace and harmony, the dead had no reason to be worried. The "Land of Promise," the "Land of Youth," or the "Isles of the Blessed" as the otherworld was sometimes called, was almost perfect in its purity. And yet, inconsistency was an important characteristic of the Celtic otherworld.

Otherworld, Tír na n-Òg, Isles of the Blessed

From the Celtic point of view there was no contradiction in the fact that the otherworld—called by the Celts of Brittany Tír na n-Óg (Isles of the Blessed)—was to be found on the other side of the sunset in the West, and at the same time was exactly where the individual Celt was living at that moment.

The famous silver Gundestrup cauldron shows how the Celts perceived life after death. Fallen warriors were placed head first into a large cauldron by the god Dagda in order to be brought back to life.

One panel of the famous Gundestrup cauldron, an enormous silver vessel dating from the 1st-2nd century BC, displays the Celts' image of life after death. The god Dagda placed fallen soldiers in an enormous cauldron headfirst in order to bring them back to life.

Halloween can be traced back to the old Celtic celebration of Samhain. Taking place during the last night of October, the living and the dead can easily contact each other. Gruesome carved pumpkins provide a scary atmosphere.

For the Celts, ordinary life took place only in people's minds, and had nothing to do with actual reality. The essential substance of life was invisible. That which people thought they was seeing was only an illusion. Bran is one of the main figures in Irish literature. Stories of his adventurous voyage across the sea were already documented as early as 700 AD.

Summation of the Celtic vision

The Celtic paradise, if one could call it that, is in a curious way similar to that of Islam—the descriptions resemble each other in many ways. The otherworld has been painted by poets and visionaries in vivid colors, showing us a land where time and death are powerless. It is a land filled with rich treasure, where nature provides enough for all without anyone having to work for it.

That which is important and good for the living is always recognizable in conceptions of the hereafter. Nourishment is available in abundance—apparently our forefathers were always struggling with lack of food and poor harvests. That problem would be solved for eternity in the hereafter.

The Celts were absolutely convinced that they would one day reach the otherworld. There would be no punishment for bad deeds, no day of reckoning along the lines of Christian beliefs. And although a monster or two might show up upon occasion, that was nothing to be alarmed about.

Originally valkyries were death demons that chose which warriors were to die on the battlefield. In later times they became supernatural warriors who fatefully governed the outcome of the battle.

THE TEUTONS

Teutonic burial rites

When a Teuton died, his eyes, nose, and mouth would be sealed with various materials, for example clay or loam.

One of the things that was forbidden was to carry the deceased directly through the house door, over the threshold. Instead, the body had to be pulled under the threshold or carried through a hole made in the wall for that purpose. Those who broke these rules would have to reckon with the dead person's revenge, often over several generations.

The body was cremated or buried in a grave. Burial findings show that brave warriors and kings were not only buried with their weapons and favorite dog, but their favorite wives were also buried alive with them in the burial mound.

As the door to the grave was closed, the woman drew her last breath in the arms of her beloved: "O commander of legions, I will sleep in your arms as I did with my living lord and sovereign." (7)

Straw death, valkyries and the god Odin

The Teutons believed in a special place in the hereafter that was only for the souls of fallen warriors. Only those who had lost their lives in battle were allowed into the warrior's paradise of Val-hall, more commonly known as Valhalla, where their bravery and loyalty would be rewarded. Nothing else mattered; there was no list of sins, no day of reckoning, only death in battle was all that was necessary to reach Valhalla. On the other hand, those who had died a dishonorable "straw death" on their sleeping pallet of straw would land in the dark and misty underworld of "Hel." The honorably deceased Teutonic warrior, or *einherjar*, would be taken from the battlefield by virginal warrior goddesses, the valkyries, to Valhalla. This was the god Odin's magnificent hall in Burg Gladsheim with 540 doors through which 800 *einherjar* standing shoulder to shoulder could pass at one time. The roof of the hall was made of shields supported by rafters made of spears. Odin lived in the castle with his wife, Frigg.

Valhalla and the drinking horns of plenty

During the day in Valhalla, brave warriors would compete in individual combat or hunt a mythical boar that was reborn every evening. At night they would sit in the great hall of the castle and feast on the divine pork, while the valkyries poured a never-ending supply of mead into their drinking horns. What the *einherjar* did apart from that is unknown. The god Odin sat at the head of the banquet table, where he and the warriors enjoyed the eternal battle that determined the destiny of gods and man alike.

No soul, just memories of the living

An important key to understanding the Teutonic death cult is the concept that the soul does not leave the body after death. To be more exact, there was no soul in the Teutonic belief as understood in the Christian occident. The dead lived on through their deeds, their children, and their fame. Most important for the Teutons was what the deceased had accomplished in life. He could only live on through the memory of others. That is why the Teutons didn't think of the grave as their final resting place. There wasn't any connection between the grave and the soul in the hereafter. Such an idea was inconceivable to the

Odin, or Wotan, was the main god in Teutonic mythology. He had widely varying roles and forms: the god of poetry, the god of death and war, the god of magic, runes and of ecstasy. Odin received the dead heroes in Valhalla.

Teutons. Those who died continued to live in their bodies, admittedly under different circumstances. Even in cases where the corpse had been burned, the body as such was indestructible.

The largest Viking burial grounds in Scandinavia contain over 600 graves. They often buried the dead in boot shaped graves. Ran, goddess of death, greeted the souls upon their arrival in her watery realm.

Cremation wasn't unknown among the Teutons. Particularly the walking dead, or *draugar*, could only be destroyed through fire. Their ashes were then thrown into a river or the sea.

Draugar and the walking dead

Not all of the dead rested in peace. Some returned and appeared to the living as the "walking dead" (not to be confused with the "living dead" of Slavic folk tales), or *draugar*. They suffered from hunger and thirst and were afraid of being cold and wet. The physical appearance of the *draugar* was in accordance with the manner of their death. Those who had been drowned were dripping wet, a man beaten to death had bloody wounds, and those who had been hung bore the marks of the noose around their necks. *Draugar* could only be destroyed by opening their grave and removing the body, cutting off the head, placing it on the buttocks, and then burning the corpse. The ashes were then thrown into the sea or a river.

Although terrifying for the living, these figures were an important source of wisdom and information about the future. The dead could be used as intermediaries between the different realms and times of reality. However, they could only be forced to foretell the future through magic, as they seldom divulged the information voluntarily.

Shape changers

The Teutons didn't share any of today's concepts of human personality. They did not speculate about what made up their individual "self," or how their personal identity differed from that of other people.

Therefore it was possible for them to believe that two people could share the same life. Their proverbs illuminate this idea. If a father and his daughter died on the same day, it was said that "they had but one life of a man between them." Another example is that Odin could transform his shape; at times he was a bird or a fish, while his body lay empty as if dead.

Loki, too, the Teutonic god of fire, appears in various guises. According to Teutonic beliefs, certain human beings also had this power to change form, sometimes even being extended to entire clans.

The idea of werewolves, that is, people who are transformed into savage animals during the night of a full moon, stems from these beliefs.

Ran, ruler of the drowned

The northern Teutons believed in a death goddess who especially took care of those who had drowned. She was called Ran, and was the wife of the sea god Aegir according to Eddic mythology. The Poetic Edda is the most important extant source on Norse mythology and Germanic heroic legends.

When someone drowned in the sea, they fell literally "into the hands of the goddess Ran." Her realm of the dead was thought to be at the bottom of the sea, where those who drowned were gathered. By her husband Aegis, she gave birth to nine daughters, who as children of Aegis were identified with the ocean waves.

Aegis himself was thought to be a kind and wise giant, whereas Ran fished the drowned souls out of the sea with a net, preventing them from reaching either Hel or Valhalla. She represented the dark and menacing aspect of the ocean. The etymology of the German word for stealing, *rauben*, can be traced back to the word Ran.

Hel, goddess of the underworld

The goddess Hel lived in the underworld in the deepest depths of the earth. Representative of her realm of the same name were the great halls where she received the dead who were not taken as warriors to Valhalla.

The golden bridge to the underworld was guarded by the giantess Modgud. The dead crossed the bridge past the hellhound Garm. Garm would allow the dead to enter Hel, but would never let them return. No sunlight ever reached the halls of Hel. The walls of the halls were formed from snake bodies, while poisonous rain ran in through the roof vents.

The dragon Nidhogg fed on the corpses of dead criminals. Hel is described in the mythology as half black, half pale as well as fierce and dismal. The English word "hell" and the German word *Hölle* were both derived from the word *Hel*. Some researchers doubt that there actually was a concept of hell in pre-Christian times. In their opinion, the Teutonic underworld wasn't personified by a goddess. The goddess Ran proves, however, that there was just such a personification in Norse mythology and in the beliefs of those times.

Those who were hanged might experience even more horror. After hanging, the limbs were hacked off the corpses. According to superstition, the dead might otherwise be able to climb out of their graves.

THE HEREAFTER IN THE MAJOR RELIGIONS

JUDAISM AND CHRISTIANITY

Judaic Sheol, land of no return

Christianity's roots lie in Judaism, and the Jews of that time period also believed in the hereafter. The barren, dark place underneath the earth to which the dead were drawn is called Sheol. *Sheol* is a Hebrew word that means hereafter, the "imperceptible," but the term is also used for grave, crypt, or realm of the dead. The hereafter was a place of putrefaction, a realm of darkness and disorder, to which both rich and poor, master and slave, king and prince, the great and the lowly went when they died. The dead are nothing more than feeble shadows, as in the ancient Greek and Roman views. Sheol was a land from which there is no return, as can be gathered from ancient texts: "the maggot is spread under thee, and the worms cover thee."(8)

We find no mention, however, of any resurrection of the dead, although God Yahweh is active in the background as Lord over life and death—and is therefore also Lord over Sheol.

In the Second Book of Kings, the prophet Elijah is "taken up" into Heaven; he experienced ascension. This Old Testament concept formed the basis of the later resurrection belief in Christianity. Right up to the present day, the concept of an afterlife does not play a role in Judaism itself, since the coming of the Messiah in this world is still anticipated. After this event, God's kingdom in this world will be permanent.

The Jews' belief in the coming of the Messiah has remained firm for millennia. With his advent, God's dominion over the world will finally begin and Jerusalem will be the eternal city of this heavenly kingdom.

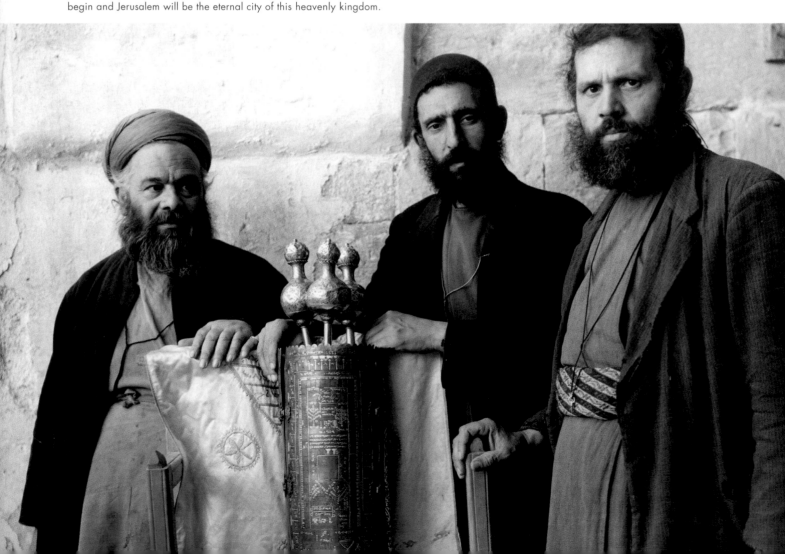

The expectation that the Messiah would appear shortly was especially widespread at the time of Jesus. The Jew Jesus called himself the One sent by God who guarantees the salvation of the people.

Resurrection and apocalypse in Judaism

Jewish belief regarding the dead, who can no longer praise God and lead a shadowy existence in Sheol, changed only very slowly. God allows only the just to rise from the dead, as indicated in the Psalms of Solomon. The godless remain in a state of eternal death. However, not all Jews believed in resurrection. Both the New Testament and the Roman author Flavius Josephus (ca. 70 AD) testify that the Sadducees (a Jewish sect friendly to Rome) did not believe in the resurrection; the Pharisees, however, did. The Jewish apocalypse basically changed the concept of an eternal place of damnation for everyone, Jewish or not, by developing the concept that worldly events unfold according to God's plan. At the center of God's plan, however, stand the Jewish people.

Jesus of Nazareth and the Kingdom of Heaven

The expectation that the promised Messiah would appear soon was especially widespread in the time in which Jesus lived. At that time, a plethora of prophets and self-appointed Messiahs were preaching in Jerusalem and other places. The Jew Jesus called himself the One sent by God who guarantees the salvation of the people. In doing so, he also openly criticized the misconduct of both the faithful and the rabbis of his day. His teachings emphasize a direct and heartfelt relationship between God and humankind based on the foundations of Judaism. His comments on the Kingdom of God, his Father's heavenly kingdom, which can be found among the people, are quite explicit in one point: the Kingdom of Heaven will become a reality already in this lifetime for anyone who believes in Jesus and his message. The divine and the human merge in Jesus von Nazareth—he agitates the world of the hereafter, in particular by raising the dead, thereby making it commensurate with this world. As religious rebel and messianic prophet he received the Roman death penalty of his day—crucifixion—at the behest of his own people.

The resurrection of Jesus is the central point of Christian theology. Jesus has risen again from the dead for all people who believe in him. This world and the hereafter are thereby no longer absolute opposites.

Rising from the dead

So, Jesus was crucified and died. But then something decisive happened: Jesus didn't remain dead, but rose again to life after three days. His body was transfigured (the body of the resurrected, not of this world) so that the first person at his grave—Mary Magdalene—did not recognize him at first, and even took him to be the gardener. However, before long his adherents were sure that Heaven and Earth, this world and the hereafter, God and humankind had been reconciled in a new and cataclysmic way through Jesus' resurrection.

What is more, the first Christians firmly believed that the resurrected Jesus, who later ascended into Heaven, would soon return. This return was called the parousia, or "Second Coming." The Apostle Paul also prophesied that the Lord would come, during his lifetime yet, on celestial clouds to lead all Christian communities into his heavenly kingdom. This world and the hereafter would then be one and the same, and God would be one with his creation in eternal happiness.

Parousia and the Last Judgment

Parousia, the Second Coming of Christ, has not yet occurred. When it did not happen during the lifetime of the Apostle Paul, the evangelist John, author of the apocalypse, spoke of a period of a thousand years. Until then, the dead should rest in their graves and joyfully await the forthcoming resurrection. At least, this was to be the case for all those who had been baptized. The resurrection of the flesh is closely connected to the Final Judgment, at which time God will exact retribution from sinners, who cannot escape their just punishment.

The origins of Hell

The present-day Christian concepts of Heaven and Hell did not exist in such a pronounced form initially. In the Gospel of John there is a reference to a "world above" that is the home of God and his heavenly hosts, the angels.

Eternal torment in the heat and darkness of Hell awaits the sinner. The Christian concept of Hell is partly borrowed from the Ancient Greeks' concept of Hades and the Jewish concept of Sheol.

The term *Gehinnom* or *Gehenna* exists in Judaism, referring both to a specific valley that actually exists near Jerusalem, the Hinnom Valley, as well as to a place of eternal damnation.

This concept also includes *Sheol*, whereby many translators of the New Testament have equated the terms *Sheol* and *Gehenna* with the Greek Hades.

For example, when Jesus says in the Gospel of Matthew 11:23, "You, Capernaum, who are exalted to Heaven, you will go down to Hades. For if the mighty works had been done in Sodom which were done in you, it would have remained until this day," he does so only to demonstrate that they will be eternally damned, and to emphasize the contrast to Heaven.

The concepts of Heaven and Hell, or the hereafter, were rather vague in the early years of Christianity, and were not as pronounced as they would later become during the Middle Ages, when they were formulated with an almost cruel delight. This naturally contributed to people's efforts to free themselves from their sins before death, for example, by making donations to the Church.

Waiting for Jesus' return

The longer the wait for the Second Coming, the more concrete the concept of eternal life became. Paradise would be an eternal place where the joys of earthly life would be greatly exceeded .

Unfortunately, the Church greatly overstated the expectations of paradise during the Middle Ages. Social injustices were often approved of, because it was especially the poor who would receive recompense in paradise for injustices suffered. It is precisely such excessive concepts of Paradise that were justly the subject of the young Karl Marx's criticism in his role as a social reformer.

Paradise degenerated into a symbol of complete gratification—an eternal place in which all are equally wealthy, equally young, and equally content. It became a wonderful instrument for drawing the sting of totally unacceptable conditions here on earth: those in authority, the Church and the aristocracy, may be living in the lap of luxury, but do not grieve, o poor Christian! in paradise we will all be equal.

Death in medieval Christian thought

In Christian belief death means the separation of body and soul. However, this separation is only temporary, because at the end of time, the body and soul will be reunited. God's judgment will then separate the good from the bad, and either reward or punish the dead accordingly.

A description dating from the year 1522 describes death's arbitrary activity as the cruel Grim Reaper. Death in the form of the skeletal Grim Reaper is neither meek nor merciful. God appears to have no control over him whatsoever. It is said that death knows neither pity nor compassion and makes no exceptions. He comes to take each and every person, tearing them away from life to a place of darkness, void of light and sun. The soul is separated from body during this act, but curiously, the medieval text does not explain what happens to the soul.

Death is the dark grave to which the person concerned is brought—no Paradise, no Purgatory, but also no Hell. The only salvation lies in the prospect of a distant judgment after leading a Christian life that has been pleasing in the sight of God.

The doctrine of Purgatory

About 200 years earlier, Pope Benedict XII (1285–1342) formulated a doctrine according to which souls that do not require purification accede to God right away, without the Last Judgment. On the other hand, evil souls are thrown straight into eternal Hell. The limited periods of catharsis and purification of other souls in *purgatorium* (Latin, "Purgatory") and the preparation there for ascension to Heaven remained. However, the concept of a Last Judgment has never fully disappeared from ecclesiastical thought. Martin Luther (1483–1546) himself longed for the end of the world by which a new, otherworldly person is created, a person lacking all earthly frailties who, fitted with a splendid body, will be immortal. Then, according to Martin Luther, God will be all in all.

Purgatory is a medieval concept. Pope Benedict XII formulated the doctrine by which the souls of those who have not sinned too seriously are sent there for purification.

Dante: Hell, Purgatory, Paradise

The famous Italian poet Dante Alighieri (1265–1321) made the hereafter the theme in his major work, *The Divine Comedy*. In it he depicts his journey, guided by the Latin poet Vergil, through Hell, to the mountain island of Purgatorio (Purgatory), and finally to Paradise.

Both Hell and Paradise are divided into concentric circles. The nearer one comes to the center, the more sinful or saintly are the souls of the deceased who reside there.

During his journey, all the people Dante meets are just the same as they were in their earthly lives; their characters have not changed. Dante depicts the abundance of the profane in the world of the dead. The here-and-now and the hereafter belong together like night and day. Dante's total universe, consisting of the here-and-now, the hereafter, and the heavenly bodies on their circuits, is spherical. On one point of the surface is the entrance to Hell, and diametrically opposite is Paradise. The whole is overarched by the nine spheres of the heavenly bodies, above which a tenth heaven is set, the home of God and origin of all creative power. (9) Nothing and no one can escape this divine creative power. It is omnipresent in Dante's world of the hereafter.

A layered world

The hereafter and the present are described both horizontally and vertically. The dead dwell above and below one another in their respective places and remain forever bound to the divine force. Dante describes Hell as a funnel with nine circles of punishment; this is the famous "Dante's Inferno," painted in a wonderfully gruesome way by Bartolomeo di Fruosino (1366–1441) around 1420. People herd together in the tightest of spaces in the realm of the dead. In Purgatory the souls have to be painfully rid of their sins, while in the glittering starry palaces of Paradise the saved and saintly live eternally in abundant light.

Since medieval times, death has readily been depicted as the Grim Reaper who cuts people down just as ripe grain is harvested. Death is also pictured as an immortal skeleton, requiring neither air nor food and drink.

The famous Italian poet Dante made the hereafter the central theme of his major work, *The Divine Comedy*. In this tripartite book he depicts in great detail a journey though Hell, to Purgatory and beyond to the paradise of Heaven.

Jesus' final return at the end of time is called Parousia. It is associated with the Last Judgment, during which evil-doers are punished and those who do good rewarded. Eternal communion with God awaits the just.

Current Christian expectations of the final days

As in the past, the various Christian churches—Catholic, Protestant, Anglican, and Orthodox—continue to await the Parousia, the final return of Jesus that he himself foretold. However, more than two thousand years later, the Second Coming has not yet happened, and the Kingdom of God in all its richness has not yet dawned, which is no simple matter when interpreting Christian doctrine. Christian expectation of the Final Days is twofold, affecting both the future Church and the fate of the individual in the hereafter, the Kingdom of God. The concrete form that this kingdom will take remains somewhat vague in the concept of the Church.

The prospect of salvation, perfect bliss for all, is in the meantime also propagated in secular social utopias. They represent an alternative for non-believers to the views of the churches. For Christians, eternal life is reflected in present-day theology not as a contrast to earthly existence, but in living in close communion with the Savior and Redeemer.

Eternal communion with God at the end of time

For Christians, Heaven consists of a close communion of believers with God and the saints that is no longer marred by the problematic nature of earthly existence. Individuals will thereby be able to fully develop their talents and be happy. The Church has parted with the concept of the hereafter as a possibility for a life directly following death. A hereafter as described by many primitive peoples and ancient religions does not exist as such in the theological understanding of the churches. Instead, belief rests more in the following: the dead fall into a kind of slumber of the soul and remain in this

a protection and support for the dying person during resurrection. A hymn for the moment of death may be sung: "Saints of God come to his aid, hasten to his side you angels of the Lord, receive his soul and bring it before the countenance of the Almighty." (10) In earlier times, to the accompaniment of the singing of psalms, the dead person was washed, dressed, and bedded on a bier, then later taken by procession to the church. This is also accompanied by singing: "You ordained that I be born, O Lord! You have promised that I will be resurrected, may the saints come at your command. Do not desert me, for you are true." (10)

All life is transient, and death and burial await each and every one of us. The hope that God will come get the dead in the future is important for believers. Until then, the deceased remain in a kind of slumber.

Belief in reincarnation in the Christian West

Two thirds of the world's population believes in reincarnation or rebirth. The concept of "re-materialization in the flesh" (a literal translation of *reincarnation*) was widespread in early Christianity, as well.

It appears that the doctrine of reincarnation was treated by the early Christians as a secret tradition not to be revealed to laypeople, and was only handed down to the select. Origen of Alexandria (185–254), an influential church teacher, explained that the souls already existed before the creation of the material world: "We are joined to lead ever new and ever better lives, be it on Earth or in other worlds. Our devotion to God, which cleanses us of all evil, means the end of our rebirth."(11) For Origen, the meaning of life was the purification of the soul through many incarnations, so that we can once again attain communion with God. However, this teaching was subsequently rejected. Many of Origen's writings were burned and, in the fourth century, Christian doctrine was finally purged of every mention of transmigration of the soul by the emperor Constantine.

state until the Last Judgment. For Catholics, especially, however, Purgatory remains as a possibility of purging oneself of evil before the Last Judgment.

Sacramental support at death

The Christian believes that the Creator both gives life and also ends it. A Catholic on the threshold of death receives the Eucharist (communion) one last time; it is

The Devil is a fallen angel who was cast down to earth because he rebelled against God. His fellow rebels were also cast down with him. Angel and devil constitute opposite poles.

Assistance from divine messengers

Angels, from the Latin word *angelus*, "messenger," can be found in both the Old and New Testaments. It was they who expelled Adam and Eve from the Garden of Eden, and they announced Jesus' resurrection from the grave. Angels were created by God as spirit beings, are representatives of Heaven, and serve as God's intermediaries with people. Their home is the various levels of Heaven from where they are sent out to bring His messages to people. Angels who have fallen away from God are called demons. They congregate around their leader, Lucifer, who was once the most splendid of all angels, but was later cast out after rebelling against the Creator.

Angels protect, rescue, and shield people, but also implement divine judgments when people seriously misuse their freedom of will.

Classifying the Angelic Hosts

Since the fifth century, the angelic choirs have been divided into three levels with a total of nine classes, whereby the seraphim, cherubim, and thrones belong to the highest level. First level: seraphim, cherubim, thrones; second level: dominions, virtues, and powers; third level: principalities, archangels and angels. The most important archangels are Raphael, Uriel, Michael, and Gabriel, who can all be found in both Jewish and Christian beliefs, while Michael and Gabriel are also found in Islam. Although angels serve Jesus with their talents and capabilities, they also lend their support to people who are dying or who find themselves in dangerous situations. Angels accompany the dead on their journey through the darkness of death to God. This concept can already be found in the story of Lazarus in the New Testament, in which angels carry the dead man into the lap of Abraham. Lazarus is this man, who is restored to life by Jesus.

The archangel Michael is Christianity's most famous angel. Many important places are named for him, such as Mont St. Michel in France. Michael revealed to Maria that she would bear a son.

ISLAM

Mohammed, Allah's prophet

The very beginning of Islam is accompanied by wondrous events. Mohammed was called by Allah to be his prophet in the cave of Hira, near Mecca, shortly before Ramadan—but his selection was not entirely voluntary. With more or less gentle force, he was moved by Allah through the angel of revelation, Gabriel, to carry out his task. In a vision, God "descended" upon his messenger like the break of dawn. Mohammed composed large parts of the Koran, and the Islamic Book of the Dead is also ascribed to him. Central to this religion is that Allah is not only the greatest, but also the one and only God.

Islam means something akin to "submission," and believers must submit themselves in all thoughts and deeds to their god. However, submission also means hope and trust in what is to come. A believer should demonstrate humility and comply with the command to strive for God. Mohammed died in 632, having founded a strong faith that is very much alive today; in fact, it is the second largest religion in the world.

Last Judgment and the dawn of the hereafter

Similar to Christianity, the revelations of the Koran state that God will hold a court of judgment in the Final Days. Until then souls remain in a place that is not further described, potentially being subjected to punishment in the grave by angels. The real hereafter literally breaks into our world for the first time with the Last Judgment, destroying it forever. The seas will rise, the sun will darken, the stars will fall on the Earth, and the sky will disappear. God is the focal point of this Day of Judgment, and only Mohammed can effectively intercede for sinners. As punishment, sinners must eat fruit that is "like liquid metal and boil like hot water in the stomach." (7)

This picture depicts Mohammed's ascension into Heaven. The face of the Prophet is not shown by the artist because Islam forbids depiction of Mohammed's facial features.

Entering Paradise

In contrast to the sinners, on this day all other believers will "have radiant faces that look upon their Lord," for they are entering Paradise, which is described in very earthly terms. The Arabic word for paradise in the Koran is *janna*. Paradise means life in a garden where rivers flow with life-giving water, trees provide shade, and the inhabitants recline on jeweled divans, in pleasant light, eating an abundance of delicious foods.

Houris, or virgins, who pleasure the men in paradise are mentioned exactly four times in the Koran and have led to perceptions of debauchery on the part of many Christian authors.

Probably a false perception

Scholars have long pointed out that these perceptions of the hereafter are most likely inspired by the graphic arts. It is quite possible that Mohammed saw Christian miniatures or mosaics of the Garden of Eden and understood the angels depicted in them to be young men and women. This presumption would actually be rather more suited to Islam, since that religion prescribes very strict rules for clothing. Modesty and purity are considered to be the highest principles for both sexes. Likewise, both men and women must cover their intimate regions. It is therefore most unlikely that everything should be just the opposite in Paradise; that would completely contradict the disciplined behavior observed on earth and make a mockery of it.

How do people imagine Paradise? Is it a wonderfully beautiful landscape in the peace of nature? Here no war is waged, sickness and frailty are absent, there is no conflict, and haste or hurry are unknown.

The holy book of the Moslems is the Koran. It was dictated to Mohammed over a long period by an angel. Mohammed then passed on what he had heard, setting down the Koran in writing, bit by bit.

Gigantic scales and the razor-thin Sirat Bridge

Whosoever has not sinned need have no fear on God's Day of Judgment. All others will be weighed on gigantic scales: on the one side are placed all the sins a person committed, and on the other lies a minute piece of paper on which is stamped the Islamic profession of faith. But the most severe test is posed by crossing the Sirat Bridge, which is said to be thinner than a hair and sharper than a sword. Anyone who prematurely ends the crossing falls into the fires of Hell, where spirits force red-hot chains into their mouths and pull them back out from their rectums. This and other unpleasant concepts of the dawn of the hereafter are described in Islamic texts such as the Book of the Dead. By contrast, Islamic poets and mystics, such as Mohammad Iqbal, have stated: "Eternal life is real life, meaning a spiritual experience, ever deepening anew, in the unfathomable depths of the Divine." (13)

False promises for suicide attackers

In an interview, Hamas activist Mohammed Abu Wardeh described how he recruited terrorists for suicide attacks in Israel. He told them how Allah compensates martyrs when they sacrifice their lives for their country: God bestows on each of them 70 virgins of paradise, 70 wives, and eternally lasting bliss.

The spokesman for Hamas used the word "martyr" (*shahid*) quite purposefully, for suicide is prohibited in Islam. Allah severely punishes all who lay hands on themselves. Martyrdom, however, is praised, embraced, and demanded. But which form does reward take in the paradise of Islam? Both the Koran and other traditional texts describe it in all its sensual details. In verses 12–39 of Sura 56 we read the following: "In gardens of delight, they shall recline on jeweled couches face to face, and there shall wait on them immortal youths with bowls and ewers and a cup of purest wine … And theirs shall be the dark-eyed houris, chaste as hidden pearls …"

The "wheel of rebirth," or samsara, turns unremittingly as long as people continue to be reborn.

HINDUISM AND BUDDHISM

On the preta condition of the soul

When Indo-Germanic nomads entered the Indus Valley around the middle of the second millennium before the present era, they brought with them the Vedic religion that later formed the basis of Hinduism. However, its oldest document, the Rigveda, a collection of hymns, provides only scarce information about the concept of the hereafter at that time. What we do know can be explained in brief: after the cremation of the body, the soul assumes an intermediary condition known as

preta. During this period it tarries on earth as a spirit, waiting to be admitted to the world of the ancestors. En route to the realm of the dead, dangerous waters have to be crossed and the hounds of the goddess of death, Yama, passed by. Eternal life, restoration of the body, exquisite foods, and musical entertainment in gregarious company await the new arrival to the realm of the ancestors.

Description from the Rigveda

In the Rigveda we read: "Where light is perpetual, in the world in which the sun is placed, in that immortal imperishable world place me … where these great waters are, there make me immortal … Where wishes and desires are, where the region of the sun is, where food and delight are found, there make me immortal! …" (5)

The Rigveda, passed on orally for centuries before it was written, dates from ca. 1200 BC and consists of ten books. In total, 1028 hymns are dedicated to various deities, for example, Indra, the patron god of warriors. The Rigveda tells us that the joys of the hereafter are only meant for those who have led a good life. Wrong-doers will be thrown into a hellish world characterized by its pitch-black darkness. Nothing is known about potential punishments there.

Rebirth/reincarnation

It was later, and after many intermediary stages, that the doctrine of reincarnation asserted itself, deciding the nature of future life within the eternal cycle of karma-samsara (good and evil deeds having a direct effect on the following life); the reborn existence is determined by the knowledge and deeds of its former life. The possibility of freeing oneself from this cycle is available for only very few. It is described in the Bhagavad Gita, one of the central documents of Hinduism, as a merging in Vishnu, who together with Brahma and Shiva forms the highest level of deities. However, those not freed linger in a place that reflects their former lives, and await their renewed return to

Brahma, Shiva, and Vishnu constitute the three-fold deity in Hinduism. Vishnu is considered to be the sustainer of the world and intervenes in the world's affairs through various incarnations. His most familiar embodiment is as the god Krishna.

this world. Wrong-doers find themselves subjected to the pains of Hell: "the dead person in his new body is drawn, with a noose around his neck and in chains, along the long desolate way to the realm of the dead while being subject to insults and blows from torture hammers. The wind from burning forests dehydrate him over red-hot sand, he is tormented by hunger and thirst." (14)

A more blissful domain for the good

In contrast to the fate of wrong-doers, which is de-scribed as dreadful the whole world over, the fate of the good sounds more pleasant: "To the south of the Nila Mountain and on the northern flank of Mount Meru lies the blissful domain of the Uttarakurus, which is inhabited by those who have accomplished perfection. There, there are sweet-fruit bearing trees that continually bloom and bear fruit; the entire ground consists of jewels and fine golden sand. The people are free from sickness, free from pain, and always happy." (14) However, both the blissful and the iniquitous conditions in the afterlife are only temporary. For, since the Wheel of Life turns for both man and god alike, rebirth follows after a brief tarry.

Indra, lord of war and master over thunder and storms, is the highest deity of the Vedic writings. As defender of the Good, he battles the forces of Evil.

The moment of death

The Bhagavad Gita provides clear advice to the living concerning the situation that confronts them at the moment of death: "At the moment of death, when the person leaves the body, his consciousness must completely merge in me (Vishnu) in parting. Then he will be united with me. That is certain. Make a regular custom of practicing contemplation, and do not let your mind wander when doing so. This way you will merge with the Lord, with him who provides light and is the highest of all." (14)

The Lesser Vehicle and the Greater Vehicle

In the original permutation of Buddhism, the possibility of salvation was limited to only very few people; hence it is known as the Lesser Vehicle—Hinayana. Mahayana Buddhism, a form that emerged around the time of Christ's birth, is known as the Greater Vehicle—Mahayana—since it opens up the possibility of salvation to a wider mass of people.

Buddha—"The Enlightened One" (ca. 560 BC–ca. 480 BC)—was born as Prince Siddharta Gautama in the house of Prince Suddhodana in Lumbini, situated in the border region between India and Nepal.

This message is important because it makes contemplation or meditation, by which all unnecessary thoughts are eliminated, the cornerstone for merging with the divine.

But that is not all. According to the original teachings of Buddha, freedom from the cycle of rebirth is achieved by self-salvation and by attaining Nirvana, a path that is open only to few.

This was combined with a broadly abstract concept of what ultimately lay in store for whoever attained it, and as a result bore the title of Buddha. "After the abandonment of happiness, the abandonment of suffering and the earlier demise of feelings of comfort and feelings of discomfort, the monk achieves the fourth level of contemplation: and remains in this complete purity of equanimity and mindfulness, without suffering, without joy." (14) The final condition is by no means to be equated with the elimination of being—such views were already rejected at an early stage.

The Land of Bliss with 3,600,000 rays of light

With the Greater Vehicle of Mahayana Buddhism, the paths of salvation are open to every true believer. All living beings should help one another along the road to deliverance from the Wheel of Rebirth.

Sukhavati, the Land of Bliss or "Pureland," which is accessible to people, is portrayed in the most beautiful colors: "O Ananda, the world is blooming, rich, and it is lovely to live there. And in this world, o Ananda, there are neither hells nor cruel nature; the flowers, twigs, branches, trunks, and roots of the golden trees are of gold and the fruit are of silver … the twigs of crystal, the leaves of coral, the flowers of red pearls, and the fruit are diamonds. Each jewel lotus emits three million six hundred thousand rays of light." (15)

The third "vehicle" for escaping the cycle of rebirth and the ongoing suffering associated with it is called Tantrayana.

The best known collection of Tantric texts is the Bardo Thodol, also known as the Tibetan Book of the Dead. It describes what happens in the period between death and rebirth, the bardo.

It cannot be denied that Buddha actually lived, since several facts about his life have been confirmed. His mother is said to have died seven days after his birth.

The Dalai Lama is the spiritual leader of Tibetan Buddhists. He was forced to leave his country when Communist China occupied Tibet during the 1950s and took action against the religion there.

A new Dalai Lama is found by showing a baby or small child items of his predecessor mixed together with articles not belonging to him. It is said he will remember the correct items and reach for them.

The secret knowledge of the Tibetan Book of the Dead

Whereas the Egyptian Book of the Dead gives an account of the gods judging souls, which are usually found to be too heavy when their sins are weighed, the Tibetan Book of the Dead (Bardo Thodol) relates in detail the soul's experience at death, in the condition that follows death (bardo), and during rebirth. While the Egyptian gods can be outwitted concerning the degree of punishment to be experienced in the afterlife, in the Bardo Thodol, souls are piteously naked in the face of the dangers and events in the realm of the dead, and are victims of their own illusions.

The Tibetan Book of the Dead is a grandiose guide to exposing the phantoms of the hereafter and their effects on the human spirit.

The Wheel of Rebirth and fear of death

In addition to the Wheel of Life, the Buddhist understanding also includes the Wheel of Rebirth. The aim of the religion is to break the cycle of becoming and decaying, as the Tibetan Book of the Dead illustrates. Where does the knowledge it contains about the condition after death come from?

Tibetans are convinced that a few people have managed to remember the events that took place in the bardo, following death, and this has served as the basis for the book's text. The central theme of the Bardo Thodol is therefore the fear of dying and our inability to perceive the projections of one's own subconscious—projections that become very potent in the state after death.

For this reason, the Book of the Dead accompanies the deceased (or dying) in the form of instructions, from the moment of death, through the intermediary state of bardos, right up to the moment of rebirth. This period consists of forty-nine days during which a Lama, i.e. a teacher, or a good friend, reads aloud near the dead person the text: "0 nobly-born, the time has now come for you to seek the Path into reality. Your guru has previously set you face to face with the Clear Light; and now you are about to experience it in its reality in the Bardo state, wherein all things are like the empty cloudless sky …" (16)

The calamity of the dead
In most cases, however, that is precisely what the deceased is not able to succeed in doing. If they were to turn straightaway toward this Clear Light, they would gain deliverance.

They would have torn apart the Veil of Maya, the symbol for our inability to see the world as it truly is, and would have achieved Nirvana, because all their visions would have been exposed as mere shadows of our imperfect consciousness. But in most cases, the deceased is distracted by the appearance of terrifying figures, and his or her own torments and fears lead them away from the Clear Light and into the darkness. Exactly this is disastrous for them.

The Tibetan Book of the Dead accompanies the dead in the form of instructions, from the moment of death, through the bardos, and right up to rebirth. A Lama reads aloud from it at the deathbed.

Rewarding good deeds

If the deceased had done lot of good deeds during their lifetime, they would now be armed to a certain degree. Bad deeds, on the other hand, catapult us into the hell of ignorance. It is precisely this that the Lama tries to avoid at the deathbed. The dead person's calls cannot reach his or her family. Irritated, they realize that they possess a second, fine material body which no one but the deceased can see, and which separates them from the world they knew. The dead person begins to despair, so the Lama tries to calm them: "The body you now have is called the thought-body of propensities. Whatever may now threaten you cannot harm you. You are incapable of dying. It is quite sufficient for you to know that all you see are your own thought-forms. Recognize this to be the Bardo." (16)

But the dead person's despair increases. Peaceful and wrathful deities appear before them. Many begin to torment the deceased, who tries to run away but cannot succeed. Then, when asked by the god of death whether they had been a good or a bad person they lie, whereupon "the furies of the God of Death sever his head, rip out his heart and entrails, lick out his brains, and drink his blood." (16)

Neutral karma and loka

However, there are also people with a neutral karma, in whom good and bad deeds are equally balanced, and who therefore experience a bland state in the bardo. Nevertheless, one thing is the true for all the dead: at the end of the bardo the bodies of the souls take on the color of the loka, i.e. the body in which they will be reborn. The dead have no power to decide whether they return to earth as a human or an animal. This is determined by their karma alone. However, it is difficult for an animal to gain release from the Wheel of Rebirth, as one might imagine.

Outside Mainstream Religions

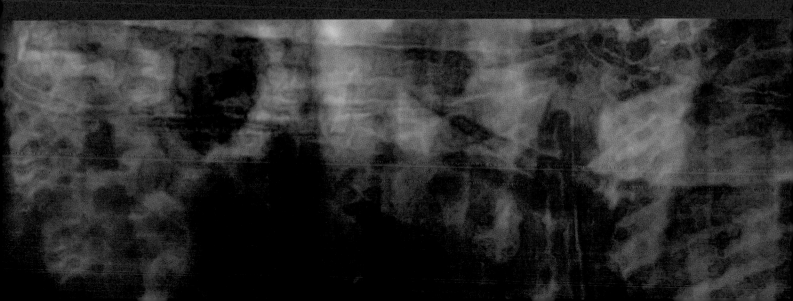

EMANUEL SWEDENBORG

Life and work as a scientist

Emanuel Swedenborg (1688–1772) initially worked as a scientist in various fields. Important discoveries that furthered research into magnetism and the atom are ascribed to him. As a doctor, he pioneered the modern science of neurology—especially through his schematic representation of brain cells, the cerebral cortex, and the spinal chord. At the same time, he also occupied himself with submarines and gliders. He later admitted in a letter to a friend that his thirty-five years of activity as a natural scientist had been a god-granted preparation for receiving the secret of life after death.

An exceptional vision

Swedenborg was fifty-seven years old when something unusual happened to him. In 1745, the highly regarded academic ended his scientific career from one day to the next. He suddenly began to take a strong interest in the occult, somewhat to the surprise of his

Emanuel Swedenborg initially worked as a scientist in various fields before devoting himself to investigating the world beyond. Inspired by a vision, he spoke of having contact with the dead.

contemporaries. However, this change had followed on the heels of a fundamental experience he had had in London. As he himself later wrote, Swedenborg saw Heaven wide open in the middle of the metropolis on the Thames. From this day onward, God allowed him free access to the world beyond and its inhabitants. Swedenborg suddenly possessed the gift of second sight and began holding conversations with spirits and angels.

The beginnings of modern occultism

The history of modern occultism begins with Emanuel Swedenborg. Never before had a seer of spirits expressed himself in writing about his "visitations." And what he communicated to his contemporaries must have shaken them to their foundations: "The souls of our fathers are by no means in a better situation than we are. Their occupations are often more lowly than

Recognition by a renowned philosopher

"A certain Mr. Swedenborg lives in Stockholm. As he himself says, his only occupation for more than twenty years has lain in the closest of dealings with spirits and departed souls, in receiving their messages from the other world and correspondingly relaying back those from this world." (17) These are the written words of none other than the philosopher Immanuel Kant (1724–1804), one of the greatest German thinkers. Kant was a contemporary of the Swedish spirit-seer, about whom he even wrote a book— "Dreams of a Spirit-Seer"—in 1766.

our own … we don't have to revere them just because they are dead. The same old problems arise, and people still have to solve them. There is no rest beyond the grave …" (18) No one there is wiser simply because they are dead.

Swedenborg also speaks of a condition similar to the Christian concept of purgatory in which the dead can purify themselves. He considers reincarnation (rebirth), by contrast, to be total nonsense and bases this opinion on various conversations with spirits. His thesis that every person is at home not only in the visible world, but also, at the very same time, in the invisible world from which we unconsciously draw our ideas and creativity. However, demons can also take hold in us when we allow them to do so. The dispositions and tendencies of these demonic forces can alter people. According to Swedenborg, the human soul partakes in Heaven and Hell. Death does not alter that significantly.

The fire of Stockholm

Swedenborg's vision of the Great Fire of Stockholm in 1759 caused a tremendous sensation when he "saw" his home city in flames over a distance of five hundred kilometers. Swedenborg was able to describe all the events that were taking place at that very moment such a great distance away with great accuracy.

He saw that his own house was in danger but would not be damaged, and declared precisely when the fire was finally extinguished.

These visions set the scientist in a frightening, state akin to possession that greatly troubled the man. But Schwedenborg was by no means considered to be mad.

One finds out everything about life and death when the heavens open, or at least mediums such as Swedenborg have claimed as much. However, there is no concrete proof, leaving everything still to conjecture.

Friederike Hauffe is regarded as the forerunner of modern spiritism by many investigators of the supernatural. Hauffe was an unusual medium. Her ability to move objects is well documented.

FRIEDERIKE HAUFFE

Investigating supernatural phenomena

A child was making soap bubbles in front of her. She said with great amazement, "O God! I can see every distant thing in this soap bubble, not small, but as big as it is in real life." (19)

More than a few investigators of the supernatural consider Friederike Hauffe (1801–1829) to have been the forerunner of spiritualist mediums associated with the phenomena of moving objects without the exertion of any perceptible external force. When someone like Hauffe receives visions by observing the mirror-like surface of soap bubbles, then it is comparable to a fortune-teller gazing into her crystal ball. Both soap bubbles and crystal balls possess a shimmering surface, which is well suited as an aid to concentration, i.e. for switching off one's own self-awareness and becoming free for perceptions from other spheres. Justinus Kerner, who observed Friederike Hauffe over a period of years, wrote a book about her and her unusual gift.

However, Friederike Hauffe's extraordinary gift also shows that such abilities can bring with them much suffering, as well.

Depression during her early years

Born 1801 in Prevorst near Heilbronn, in southern Germany, the seer was already able to sense the spirits of the deceased when she was still a child. Nevertheless, the girl was always well-balanced and cheerful,

Visions have been experienced in every time period. The prophets of the Old Testament saw God in his magnificence. Hauffe claimed to know the language spoken by heavenly beings.

How much value do the assertions of mediums have? Are they bubbles that burst when scrutinized more closely? Friederike Hauffe saw far-distant things in soap bubbles, comparable with gazing into a fortune teller's crystal ball. Was it her imagination or reality?

A language unknown to us

Much about Friederike Hauffe remains a puzzle. Among other things, she spoke in an oriental-sounding language: she used the term *emela-chan* for a spirit; *elschaddei* for God; the moon was called *schmado*; a wench *alentana*; and *dalmachan* still awaits interpretation. *Nochiane* was supposedly a nightingale. All this she said while in a trance, during which she could be asked about the meaning. When fully conscious again, she knew nothing of what had been said.

as Kerner was able to ascertain. At the age of nineteen, she moved to Oberstenfeld, a nearby community. When her parents decided it was time for her to marry, she became melancholic for a long period and hardly spoke. This depression only left her when she suddenly collapsed into unconsciousness at the funeral of an acquaintance in 1822.

Suffering in a weightless state

She was confined to her bed for eighteen weeks. Her wedding then took place when she was finally able to walk again. Shortly afterwards she became pregnant, and her suffering began anew. For twenty-two weeks she suffered from fever—accompanied by severe chest cramps and bleeding.

Her child came into the world, but died after only a few weeks. During this time Friederike saw a fiery mass around her, spoke in verses, or saw herself standing at the bed. Her teeth fell out, and she suffered alternately from attacks of fever and dysentery, in addition to continual menstruation.

Kerner writes, "she was somebody at the very moment of death, held back between life and death by some kind of fixation." (19) Then uncanny things began to happen. Objects near her began to move, spoons moved very slowly through the air, she saw her deceased grandmother and other dead people, whereby Hauffe often complained about the obstinacy of the deceased she wished to help through prayer and clarification. If one pressed one's fingers against Friederike's she would rise from the bed as if weightless.

She could foretell people's deaths, describe the dead in the hereafter, and developed a curious theory about the soul, spirit, and numbers. According to Hauffe, following death it is possible to summarize an entire life in one single number.

She never explained how she came to this conclusion. Kerner assumed it was a message "from beyond."

Friederike Hauffe's condition deteriorated visibly. It was soon obvious that her time had run out. Spirit apparitions became more numerous during the last years of her short life.

A short life of illness

Friederike Hauffe's condition visibly deteriorated, and it was soon obvious that her time had run out. Spirit apparitions became more numerous during the last years of her brief life.

In her opinion, animals live in a dream sphere, directly behind which can be found the hereafter. No one since her has ever again spoken of the hereafter in such terms. On August 7, 1829, her soul left her body—reportedly with a cry of joy.

Justinus Kerner then began to bring some order to the few intellectual things she had left behind her and published them in a book.

The right number embodies the entire being

Friederike Hauffe's deliberations sound very hermetic, although the young woman had no formal education whatsoever. She maintained that every individual is given a root number that expresses their entire being. What is more, the entire universe is comparable to a numerical system.

Everything in the universe has a certain numerical value with digits behind the decimal point. We are also told just how important the root number, unknown to the individual, is: "The individual whose number is not disturbed by anything will reach the oldest age." (19) In addition, people are unknowingly evaluated on a day-by-day basis—using numbers. She did not say who evaluates the people. The numbers rise against the individual's own root number, and decrease again. The driving forces for this are good and bad deeds, but also external influences. An individual must die when the personal number is exceeded for too long, due to external influences and bad deeds.

According to the seer, best of all is when good and bad deeds, expressed in numbers, always lie below one's own root number. After death, people see their own life clearly on the basis of the difference between the number attained and their own personal root number. One's own spirit then becomes one's judge.

EUGENIE VON DER LEYEN

The princess and the poor souls

According to the Catholic Church, "poor souls" are the deceased who are sent to a place of purification from their sins, i.e. purgatory, for a period of time after their deaths. What is meant here is more a state of being than a specific place. When the condition of the soul improves to such a degree that it is redeemed, it can enter Heaven. According to Catholic teaching, the soul then "abides" with God. This process of purifying the "poor souls" normally remains hidden from the eyes of the living.

Following the advice of her father confessor, Sebastian Wieser, Princess Eugenie von der Leyen of Baden-Württemberg (1867–1929), who as far as we know was in full possession of her mental faculties, kept a special kind of diary during the years 1921 to 1929.

In it, she describes her almost daily dealings with poor souls forced to adopt the most terrible forms as spirit beings in the cleansing fire. Eugenie von der Leyen thereby functioned as a kind of medium.

Princess von der Leyen maintained that she had gained insight into the world of the poor souls in Purgatory. She wrote how the suffering souls came to her and demanded help from her, causing her great pain.

It could also be the Devil

The often frightening appearance of the souls that visited the princess reflected the seriousness of the sins they had committed on earth. Eugenie recorded in her diary, "April 24. For three days now, an animal, a thing between a small buffalo or ram, totally black, is coming to me in the night, which is not very comfortable. It jumped on my bed. I am very alarmed, it has a human face, but totally black, scary, it could also be the Devil. Holy water helped, it soon went away." (20) A nun appeared to her as a snake, and badly afflicted her. When her form became human, interesting conversations took place.

The souls in bestial form insisted that the princess help them, she wrote. In this they expected her total

What is a medium?
Medium, Latin for "intermediary link," is the term used to describe a person who is capable of extrasensory perception and who can establish contacts to the hereafter. For centuries, this has taken place in séances, spiritualist sessions during which the medium falls into a trance, i.e. reaches a state in which they act as an empty "vessel" for spirits and extrasensory messages, and is "filled" by them.

Modern spiritism began in 1847 with a case of haunting in Hydesville, New York. There, a certain Mr. Post invented an ABC of raps in order to communicate with a dead man who had made his presence known by making noises. Mr. Post found out that the man had been murdered and discovered where his body lay hidden.

devotion in order to at least be able to take on human form. Eugenie behaved as a model Christian and was ready to help at all times. The deceased often beat, strangled, insulted, or scared the poor woman so severely in the process that she thought she could no longer bear it.

An especially unpleasant apparition

One of these figures called himself the "ape" and continued staring at her with glowing eyes every night until Eugenie's fervent prayers of intercession enabled this "impure" being to regain the power of speech. In reply to her question why he had beaten her despite her willingness to help him, he said his wish to torment her was due to his state, which knew only badness. Eugenie swore that she had never seen such a revolting thing. His body was the lair of a thousand living worms. The princess prayed and fasted for the poor souls. The princess represents the kind of devout Catholic who comes to the aid of the poor souls in Purgatory through prayer and sacrifice—a labor of spiritual charity.

An altruistic, friendly woman

Eugenie von der Leyen was a woman of rather stout stature with a fleshy, rosy face. Her hairstyle was typical of the times—she wore her long brown hair rolled

The princess wrote of a spirit she called the "ape." Every night it would stare at her with glowing eyes. Only after Eugenie's fervent prayers, was it purified and regained the power of speech.

up evenly all around, like a wreath. Everyone who knew the princess described her as a self-sacrificing, ever-friendly, and altruistic woman. No one considered her to be mad and she presumably was not. Her experiences are completely subjective and lie beyond our powers of appraisal. Eugenie also had other peculiar experiences.

She saw, for example, a deceased parish priest that she knew well, just at the moment when the verger walked straight through him in his church. She describes both as having a checkered appearance. She was able to recount numerous conversations with the spirits, word for word, from memory.

The many questions Eugenie von der Leyen asked reflected her denominational background. The almost sober way she recorded her various encounters in her diary make the experiences credibly comprehensible for the reader.

Numbers govern our lives. We know our date of birth, but most people would not care to know the date of their death. "Three times nine," Eugenie von der Leyen was told, and was none the wiser.

The face of the Devil causes fear because he is the embodiment of evil. In fact, Lucifer is a fallen angel. His name means "Bearer of Light," while Beelzebub is a translation of "Lord of Flies."

A prophecy from the hereafter

The following story is regarded as proof of the truth of her statements. On All Souls' 1925, she asked a deceased Dominican father she was friendly with about the date of her own death. The Dominican supposedly replied, "three times nine." She had no idea what he meant. To this he responded that she was not supposed to know what he meant. Princess Eugenie von der Leyen died on January 9, 1929 in the castle of Unterdießen, south of Landsberg, where she had spent the last four years of her life. The date contains the digit 9 three times. She herself had believed she would die on an August 9.

Seth was originally the murderer of the Egyptian god Osiris. In the case of Jane Roberts, Seth becomes a wise spirit being from the hereafter. He describes himself as an energy personality core that is no longer centered in physical form.

Jane Roberts was an unusual medium who first made contact with a mysterious being called Seth in 1963. In numerous séances Seth disclosed things to her that expanded her understanding of life and death.

JANE ROBERTS

A channeling medium by chance

Jane Roberts was by far the most remarkable channeling medium of the last century, by which is meant she was a medium who served as a channel for spirit beings to communicate with the living.

When she died in New York in 1984, at the young age of only fifty-five years, she left behind a great wealth of material and recordings that were dictated to her while she was in a trance state by a being from the hereafter called Seth.

Prior to discovering her special gift, Jane Roberts had attended Skidmore College in Saratoga Springs, New York. Following her graduation from college, she had been a writer of poems and narratives. Up to this point in her life, she had had no unusual experiences with extrasensory perceptions whatsoever, and was not even particularly interested in that kind of thing.

But then, in 1963, something new happened to her. Jane Roberts was in her mid-30s when out of sheer curiosity she and her husband experimented with a Ouija board.

Who is Seth and what exclusive knowledge does he have?

For Jane Roberts, Seth became a source of secret knowledge. He described himself as an energy personality core that is no longer centered in a physical form. For Seth, a person's soul is his or her true self—both highly individualized spiritual energy and multidimensional self.

Soul and consciousness exist independently from body and time and space, which is the reason they can attain a greater understanding of the cosmos and their own existence through dreams and intuitive insights. In Seth's opinion, a person must awaken his inner perception in order to see properly. Seth's messages for Jane are concerned with such themes as dying, life after death, reincarnation, God, Jesus Christ, and the cosmos.

They impart thoroughly new, interesting aspects of these topics. His statement on the difference between humans and animals is also remarkable: "You are not separated from the animals and the rest of creation by your possession of an eternal inner consciousness. Such a consciousness is present in all living beings and in all forms of being." (21)

Channeling

A spirit being with excellent knowledge introduced himself to Jane Roberts: Seth. The author and talented medium received his messages until her death, and published them in several books: *The Seth Material*, *Conversations with Seth*, and *The Individual and Mass Psyche* are just a few. This is known as "channeling," whereby, other than the dead contacted in spiritism, the truly knowledgeable personifications concerned are beings of comprehensive awareness. Theosophists would speak of beings on the last, highest sphere, immediately before God.

The Ouija board

A Ouija board represents an extension of automatic writing for people with the gift of being a medium. In automatic writing, one's own will releases complete control so that other, external beings can gain influence and convey messages.

In the case of the Ouija board, an indicator slides around on a board indicating letters to form specific words. However, according to statements by mediums, the experimentation with the letters is no longer subject to one's own will, but takes place in a trance-like state.

The results gathered in this way are evaluated differently. Spiritism sees a spirit presence as the force directing a medium's movements, while modern depth-psychology and parapsychology both surmise that the subconscious has become active here. In either case, the Ouija board can serve as an instrument for receiving messages from the hereafter.

The soul is infinite

What Seth is trying to convey is a vision of the soul as an unrestricted entity. It is the same ancient dimension of experience of the shaman who, time after time, experiences how the borders of the self can merge into the infinity of the cosmos. The world, the universe, God, and all that exists—nothing is actually separate from us.

There is a beautiful text by Omar Khayyam (1048–1122) that brings this to the point: "I sent my soul through the invisible, some letter of that afterlife to spell; and by and by my soul returned to me, and answered, 'I myself am Heav'n and Hell'." (22) Omar Khayyam was a highly regarded Iranian mathematician, astronomer, and poet of his day.

According to the information Seth imparted to us, God in his cosmos is a continually expanding and omnipresent energy, sustaining and giving expression to everything that is.

Information from Seth
Jane Roberts' supernatural spirit—Seth—provides very detailed information about the organization of and life in the hereafter. Seth appears to have an almost messianic need to point out to mortal humans that the body is only a shell for something greater. He deals with the process of dying, the "transition," as well as the theme of reincarnation. Regarding good and evil he said: "I would like ... to emphasize once more that there are no such things as devils and demons, apart from those you create for yourselves through your beliefs." (21) This statement is very clear. For Seth, God is "all-that-which-is." Dreams, various states of consciousness, and sleep at night also belong to that which he interprets within the framework of an all-embracing spirit. It is the individual's task to learn that all things in the universe are bound together.

The latest findings in astrophysics show that the cosmos is not infinite and eternal. But is the human soul immortal? Will science ever be able to prove it once and for all?

JAMES VAN PRAAGH

A highly gifted medium

For more than twenty years, James van Praagh, who lives in Los Angeles, has been giving lectures and holding workshops to pass on his knowledge of the hereafter. He is considered the best known contemporary medium in the USA. Born in New York and raised in the Irish-Catholic tradition, van Praagh originally wanted to become a priest. He soon recognized, however, that the religion fettered his special relationship to God. At the age of 24 he realized that he is a highly talented medium, and from then on saw it as his task to provide evidence for life after death. His difficulty lay in the fact that as living beings in a three-dimensional world, we negotiate our way using its language and logic, whereas a completely new "language" is required to understand the afterlife. Spirits and the dead communicate telepathically with each other on the other side of existence.

The dead in search of contact

James van Praagh had his extrasensory talents trained by a British medium. He seeks contact with the dead while in trance. Initially thoughts flow to him, then later feelings and pictures. This way he receives a vision of what the dead wish to communicate to him. Many of the bereaved are amazed at his precise knowledge of scars and birthmarks on various parts of the deceased's bodies, things he could not have known beforehand. The American medium is often asked why the dead get in touch again at all. His reply: because they wish to let their loved ones know that they are fine, that they are not actually dead, and that they now love those they have left behind even more than they did in life.

Reincarnation and alien life

James van Praagh is a stalwart of reincarnation, and he propagates a life beyond death in which the soul is not

James van Praagh is currently the best-known medium in the USA. This unusual man of Irish-Catholic upbringing lives and works in Los Angeles, where he gives lectures and holds workshops.

necessarily reborn in a human body. To make things even more complicated, van Praagh believes that an individual simultaneously possesses several bodies, which are present on different levels. Only the enlightened can perceive all of them at the same time. Our present body, bound as it is by the limitations of

three-dimensionality, appears as the heaviest and most immobile of all the bodies we possess. According to van Praagh it is "impervious to matter." By contrast, in another dimension it is so flexible that it can be present at different places at one and the same time. For van Praagh, the hereafter is similar to the quantum universe of modern physics in which all imaginable possibilities exist, where an atom can travel through two different doors at the same time, as has long been proven on an experimental level. Tests have shown that an atom can be at two different places simultaneously.

Repercussions from a previous life

Van Praagh has found out something about himself; namely, that there is a good reason why he has long been afraid of water. In a previous life, as a galley slave,

An alien as often represented in Hollywood films of the genre. Van Praagh contends that a soul can also be reborn in the body of an alien, on another planet.

Van Praagh's belief in rebirth was the result of a "regression." He recalled that he had been a galley slave in a previous life and had died during a storm. Is this the reason for his fear of water?

The difference between spirits and ghosts

Born in 1936 in Kansas City, Missouri, Sylvia Browne has been considered a clairvoyant for almost sixty years. In her book *Visits from the Afterlife* she provides a remarkable definition for making a distinction between spirits and ghosts.

She says the dead have two possibilities. Figuratively speaking, upon death they see two doors. If they go through the left-hand door, they return to an earthly womb and are reborn. If they pass through the door to the right, they enter the hereafter and are souls subject to the God-given laws of the afterlife. These inhabitants of the hereafter are called spirits.

But for Sylvia Browne there is yet a third group that wishes neither to be reincarnated nor to enter the tunnel filled by God's brilliant-white light that will lead them into the hereafter. They remain, for whatever reason, in an intermediary place and are still bound to earth.

Sylvia Browne calls these souls ghosts, and when they appear to the living one speaks of a haunting. She writes, "It can be very helpful to know the difference between spirits and ghosts, between a visitation from the hereafter and a haunting, especially when one unexpectedly comes into contact with life after death." (23)

he had piteously drowned, chained to his oars. This was recognized and overcome during a regression, which some therapists currently offer their patients. Once the reason for the phobia (excessive fear) had been clearly identified, it could then be vanquished once and for all.

James van Praagh also recognizes the concept of karma, believing that the good and evil that we do in our lives comes back to us. According to the medium, human beings should realize that death is an illusion and build our lives on a solid moral foundation.

Van Praagh on a particular question about reincarnation

The most important question that many pose in respect to reincarnation is why we have no constant recollection of an earlier life. Van Praagh counters that it is an act of grace by God. All previous existences are blanked out to give us a clean sheet in leading our current lives.

However, there are possibilities, for those who wish to identify themselves, to directly remember the previous information and parts of their karma.

MODERN CONCEPTS OF THE AFTERLIFE

Theosophists maintain that the soul can travel during sleep. Earthly matter is denser and heavier than the material of the astral body, which is therefore able to separate itself from the body.

THEOSOPHY

What does theosophy mean?

Literally translated, theosophy means "knowledge of God." Theosophy primarily considers itself to be a scientific system of investigating occult truths. It strives to investigate and awaken the spiritual powers that are dormant in people in order to overcome the limits of earthly human existence and penetrate the spheres of the afterlife.

In theosophist belief, the hereafter is constantly influencing this world because its matter is in a higher state of oscillation. The material of earthly life is denser and heavier than, for example, the matter of the astral body. Individuals are at home in both worlds and find themselves wanderers between both spheres.

The deeper individuals ensnare themselves with material things, the more we forget our true home— the bright world of the spirit. Human cravings and passions chain us to the material world. It is only upon death that we can recognize our true goal: then we are ready to cast our previous lives aside like a gown and face our true task: the development of the true, immortal being in Christ's ideal image.

It is only to our advantage that we should succeed in this during our lifetime.

Death

According to theosophist line of thinking, the fear of death is the result of materialism that is rooted too deeply. Only the insight that we are eternal spirit beings who, upon death, merely cast aside the chains of the body can relieve the horror of death. The difference between death and sleep is merely that when we fall asleep the ethereal body (soul) does not separate itself completely from the physical body, but remains connected to it by a fine, silver-bright, vibrating band—the silver cord.

This silver cord is only broken when we die. Before this takes place, the whole life of the dying person passes by in vivid pictures—in reverse, from their last moments back toward birth. When death then does take place, the deceased is surprised to find that their surroundings hardly change. They see and hear the people they have left behind, and continue to take part in their lives. Their senses and possibilities of movement are greatly enhanced.

Nevertheless, the theosophists tell us that passing on does not alter anything about the character of the individual concerned. We are all the same as we were beforehand, neither wiser nor dumber. However, the hereafter reveals itself to us only as it has already existed in our minds and imaginations: a deceased conductor therefore returns to conduct his orchestra on the day of his memorial service, just as he has always done. His senses will see the tones rising materially. All the melodies appear to him as colorful works of art.

Madame Helena Petrovna Blavatsky

The Theosophical Society is principally the life's work of Helena Petrovna Blavatsky (1831–1891), better known as Madame Blavatsky or HPB. She was a dazzling, strong personality and today many consider her the forerunner of the channeling movement. Channeling is contact between a medium and spirits of the highest order, who have great knowledge of the spirit structure of the hereafter.

Madame Blavatsky came from an old Russian aristocratic family and had traveled widely, studying voodoo rituals as well as the secret knowledge of Tibetan masters and ancient Egypt. She was both well-read and enterprising.

In 1875 she founded the Theosophical Society and published her first major work, *Isis Unveiled*. Her success was seminal from the very beginning. Many artists and intellectuals felt themselves drawn to Madame Blavatsky.

But there were also critics who accused Blavatsky of deception and manipulation during her séances, which deeply annoyed her.

In 1885 she settled in Naples, Italy, at the foot of Vesuvius, where she wrote many letters defending her views. Her second major work, *Secret Doctrine*, in which she recounted the history of mankind from a theosophist point of view, appeared in the fall of 1888. *Secret Doctrine* laid claim to being the essence of all religions, but also contains much that is racist in nature, for Madame Blavatsky talks of the good and the bad races of people.

Hell and Purgatory

Theosophy imagines the hereafter as seven distinctly pronounced spheres. Three of them belong to the lowest regions, and thus constitute the Underworld. Meanness, lust, and malice are the qualities that land someone here, and they result in a corresponding appearance. The lowest sphere is called Hell, a dark, gruesome, desolate, icy region in which devilish characters are allowed to live out their wicked natures. All three of the lowest spheres are characterized by dead beings who have gravely sinned during their lives. However, they have the possibility of ascending as soon as they recognize that there is something pure and bright beyond the gratification of their own desires. Above Hell in this scheme of spheres lies a place where souls can do penance—Purgatory.

Purgatory, a state of penance

Here the soul can do penance once it recognizes its misdeeds and repents. This is all very much in line with traditional Catholic-Christian understanding. Purgatory is a state in which the individual is made to experience all the wrong-doings they perpetrated during their lifetime. Princess von der Leyen wrote about this in her diary, as well. As soon as the strength of the committed evils and indulged vices is dissipated, and the soul repents, one is in a position to ascend further. However, there should be no misunderstanding. The possibility of slipping back again remains if the soul is in a precarious condition. It is a woeful experience. Purgatory lies between Heaven and Hell and is not a sphere as such, but rather an intermediary area, a waiting and cleansing zone—an inner state that is less than pleasant.

The Summer Land

Like Hell, the Summer Land also provides three various spheres for the dead. Blue is the dominant color here. This is why mediums also speak of the "blue world." Those who are allowed to dwell here have already been freed from their passions and

As is the case with Hell, Summer Land consists of three distinct spheres for accommodating the dead. Blue is the dominant color, which is why mediums also call it the "blue world."

desires. Bright and hopeful life, full of expectation, can be felt everywhere. According to the theosophist view of things, the scenery of the afterlife is characterized by a peaceful and staid landscape in which the dead carry out specific tasks—almost as in their earthly lives. The lowest level is populated by those who were more indifferent to the fate of their former fellow man. Practicing existence together is a compulsory daily duty here; no one can refuse to participate.

Middle region

The middle region of Summer Land is somewhat more colorful and different from the lowest levels. Here the dead imagine themselves to be in a luscious summery landscape. Those who in life cared more for their own private fancies can now be found here, freeing themselves from such obsessions. The highest region of these spheres is of incredible beauty—a perfect paradise straight out of a holiday brochure—where gardens rich in flowers and a steel-blue sea alternate with extensive fruit orchards. Animals and humans live side by side in peaceful harmony—in reality, the dead color in this wonderful state themselves. The ideal image of family and community is lived out here. Many already consider this to be Heaven, and feel no desire to ascend further. But here theosophy warns us: only those absolutely free of desires for themselves and others can pass on to the bright, selfless heavenly world. It takes great personal effort to reach such a state.

Heavenly life

Only people completely free of passions, desires, and every selfish tendency are allowed to enter the heavenly world. That may sound somewhat boring, but one should make no mistake: here, whatever the world may have to offer in pure joy is a permanent state of affairs for the soul. The dead are surrounded by an incomparable wealth of colors, shapes, and sounds. All ideals are realized; life is as wished, formed by thoughts alone. Altruistic love is the driving force behind everything. The dead strive toward the goal of the entire universe, which is to reconcile the creation with its Creator.

Only those who are completely free of passions, desires, and every selfish tendency are allowed to enter Heaven. Altruistic love is the sole driving force, with the goal of reconciling creation to God.

From the highest and purest back to Earth

Angels and other beings of indescribable beauty share this highest level with humans. Here souls live and act consciously. No comparison is capable of conveying the splendor and grandeur, the immeasurable radiance of light, the vibrant tones, and inner experiences of this state. The souls of this sphere are characterized by an awareness of union with every living and thinking thing, influenced by neither time nor space, and utterly fulfilled by the nearness of God.

Nonetheless, according to theosophy, souls that reach this highest level don't remain in this state of pure wonder and bliss. They themselves are matured, enlightened, and feel an inner urge to reincarnate once again. This is due to the imperfection of the universe. Return to an earthly existence in all its facets, both light and dark, is necessary to fulfill the plan for all of creation—the perfection of humanity on all levels of existence.

NEAR-DEATH EXPERIENCES

Raymond Moody and his discovery

Near-death experiences became widely known in the twentieth century following the publication of *Life After Life*, the bestselling first book published in 1975 by an American doctor named Raymond A. Moody.

Moody had investigated statements and reports on the subject that he had become aware of in his surrounding environment. As both a physician and a philosopher, Moody wanted to find out more about this phenomenon.

His investigations dealt with accounts related by people who had stood on the threshold between life and death and, in medical terms, had been declared dead. Today, as a result of his ground-breaking work, near-death experiences are taken seriously, and such reports are gathered from patients all over the world as part of ongoing investigations.

Raymond Moody wrote a bestseller detailing the near-death experiences of people who had apparently died. People declared clinically dead concur in reporting a better world.

Description of a typical near-death experience

Moody presented the results of his investigations in his first book, *Life After Life*, as well as others that followed. It soon became clear that the near-death experiences of many people included striking similarities. The dying people often reported hearing the doctor declare them dead. They then suddenly hear strange sounds and, at the same time, find themselves to be moving through a dark tunnel. By some miracle they find themselves outside of their bodies, yet back at the place of their death; they observe the attempts that are being made to resuscitate them. "With deeply troubled feelings, he watches the attempts at resuscitation from this strange position of observation. After a brief period, he calms down and begins to get more and more used to his strange condition. He discovers that he still possesses a 'body'" (24)—albeit changed.

People on the threshold between life and death are often greeted by beings that wish to help them. Very few people declared clinically dead speak of unpleasant encounters.

A different body and beings of light

Almost all those who have lived through a near-death experience describe their bodies as somehow altered, and possessing new capabilities. Moody formulates this as follows: the body is it was before, but "differs substantially in both its composition and its capabilities from the physical body that has been left behind." (24)

An additional experience common to many people with near-death experiences is that they encounter so-called beings of light, which appear to the dying. They are frequently the spirits of friends or relatives who have previously died and who wish to welcome or help the person dying. They are described as "beings radiating light and warmth." (24)

A review of one's life and return

These strange beings of light then address the dying person, without using words, however. Their intention is nevertheless clear to the person having the experience: they should assess their life.

The being helps them "by causing a panorama of the most important stations of his life to flash by in an instantaneous review." (24)

Almost everyone who has had such an encounter later reports that during the course of this review "he nears a kind of barrier or boundary that obviously represents the dividing line between earthly life and the life that follows. But he becomes aware that he must return to earth, that the time for his death has not yet come." (24)

Most people also remember that they felt no desire at all to return to earthly life after these experiences in the "intermediate world" because they were filled with the pleasant feelings they were experiencing in the hereafter.

"Despite his inner resistance—and without knowing how—he nevertheless rejoins his physical body and continues living." (24)

Mediums describe separation from the body as the soul drawing itself out of the body. No further obstacles bar its way once the astral body has left its mortal shell.

The most important question about the meaning of life concerns the nature of humanity. Near-death investigations can definitely contribute to finding the answer. But how valid are they?

Catalyst for further research

Anyone subject to such an extraordinary experience as just described is deeply influenced by it. All those who have had such a trenchant experience have a changed relationship to death as a result. Sometimes they turn their entire previous lives upside down. Can such serious repercussions be the result of nothing more than hallucinations and fantasies?

Many years have passed since Moody's bestseller was first published, and in the meantime various disciplines have begun investigating the phenomenon of near-death experience more closely. Numerous statements gathered have demonstrated that the phenomenon is described similarly all over the world. Investigations carried out on brain activity have not only shed light on new aspects of the phenomenon, but have also given rise to a number of remarkable points for debate. Fundamental medical— primarily neurophysiological—questions have arisen regarding death.

All these reports come exclusively from the living. Do their statements about life after death therefore have any validity?

The body's own hallucinogens— an explanation?

One theory for explaining experiences of near-death is that the visions are caused by substances produced by the body itself. We now know from research that the body produces its own opiates, releasing them in certain situations. This happens, for example, when athletes run for a long period. Uneasy with the phenomenon of near-death experience, some neurologists and doctors are looking at this as a possible explanation. Endorphins, serotonin and glutamate, combined with hypoxia (oxygen deficiency of the blood or tissue), are the primary substances suspected of being especially liable to trigger a near-death experience. In plain language, this means that when faced with impending death, the body drugs itself, so to speak, with certain powerful chemical substances in order to deceive itself with beautiful images— endogenous receptors for this have already been found in the brain.

Death as a journey of no return

It is not easy to determine when someone is dead. Brain death and cardiac arrest are the classical criteria for a definitive medical diagnosis of death, but there are questions.

Near-death experiences are affected by this insofar as they always take place prior to this definitive diagnosis. This is obvious, for anyone who crosses that point of no return cannot come back to report on their experience, the impressions gained, and the feelings experienced. Particularly theologians maintain that near-death experiences cannot give us insight into the worlds or structures of the hereafter because the person concerned has not conclusively crossed the threshold of biological death.

Theologians, in particular, maintain that near-death experience cannot provide a glimpse of the afterlife. They argue that no one has crossed the threshold of biological death.

What happens when we die? Neurologists seek an answer, and believe the body uses the opiates they've found in the brain to delude the consciousness into believing it is entering a more perfect world.

Near-death experience—a creation of specific regions of the brain?

Brain researchers such as the distinguished physician Dr. Michael Schröter-Kunhardt suspect that certain regions of the brain form the biological source of religious and paranormal experiences. There are two significant reasons for interest in the neurophysiological conditions surrounding near-death experience. One is the desire to clarify the circumstances "under which near-death experience occurs and by which it could possibly be artificially induced. This has already been achieved in the case of certain aspects of near-death experience." (25) This entailed the stimulation of the appropriate regions of the brain, and has partially achieved effects similar to "actual" near-death experiences. On the other hand, efforts are being made on the part of some researchers to attribute all near-death experiences to neurobiological functions. They are attempting to prove that these subjective experiences are nothing more than fiction, created by certain sections of the brain. For them, the brain is a kind of film producer of near-death experiences.

Consciousness beyond the limitations of the physical body

Dr. John Lorber, regarded in both Britain and the USA as an eminent expert in the field, has gathered cases in which people either had very little brain matter, or have suffered complete or partial failure of that organ as a result of a serious accident. If the results are correct, they would lead to the conclusion that the consciousness can exist without the brain—because more exists than just the physical body.

Life without a brain

The neurologist Dr. John Lorber, of Sheffield University in England, has made a sensational discovery that fits very well into this context. Dr. Lorber examined a man with a larger than average head. The patient displayed an enormous mathematical intelligence. His IQ had repeatedly been measured at 126 (a value of 100 denotes average intelligence). Accordingly, his school results had also been excellent. When he examined the man's head, Dr. Lorber was amazed to find no brain present. What Lorber found was a millimeter-thin layer of brain cells. The rest was water. The doctor justly asked himself how this man managed to remain alive. It was a medical puzzle.

The youngster Andrew Vandal, born on July 12, 1984, is another case of such an anomaly. It was discovered that a cyst had formed on his brainstem during development in the womb. This cyst had hindered the development of his brain. In plain words, this meant that the young boy's skull was filled with cerebrospinal liquid, a watery, clear brain and spinal cord fluid, instead of a brain. The boy was born despite this deformity, and adopted by Kaye Vandal from Wallingfort, Connecticut. According to medical assessment, the child should not have survived. He may not be able to speak and can only scoot while lying on his back, but he reacts to stimuli, laughs, and his mental development appears to be proceeding.

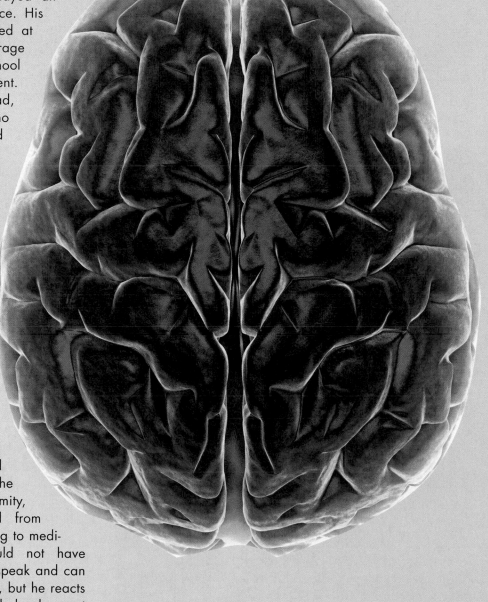

Perhaps near-death experiences really are fictions created by specific regions of the brain. However, Dr. John Lorber discovered that it is actually possible to survive with almost no brain.

Attempts at scientific explanation

It was initially assumed that opiates produced by the body itself were the primary factors involved in the occurrence of near-death experiences. And so, experiments were carried out that involved using endorphins and other substances to stimulate the regions of the brain concerned in order to induce a near-death experience. By and large this failed, because the body's own opiates already play a role in many daily situations and appear not to be sufficiently significant in the field of near-death experience. In principle, it can be said that the body's own drugs can only induce fragments of the near-death experience—which is also the case with externally administered drugs, such as marijuana.

Speculation that near-death experiences may be due to brain injury can confidently be rejected on the basis of the many reports of completely healthy people. Nevertheless, a specific region of the brain, the temporal lobe, is probably involved.

Specific regions of the brain play an important role

The temporal lobe is the lower part of the cerebrum. This is where optical impressions are processed. When electrically stimulated, it produces at least fragmentary elements of near death experience, e.g. the notion of being able to pass through solid material (a wall).

Neurobiology is primarily occupied with the structure of the nervous system. Its research has long sought to explain near-death experiences. So far, the results have proven inconclusive. Numerous phenomena could not be explained, or only inadequately. However, speculation has grown that the limbic region of the brain does play a special role in near-death experience. Most unequivocal of all is the role the limbic system plays for the memory; it integrates external and internal influences and evaluates them emotionally.

Are near-death experiences triggered by the body's own drugs? Such a theory has been formulated. Experiments have shown, however, that the body's own opiates are not specific enough to account for all aspects of near-death experience.

Research and researchers

The content of near-death experience is very much divorced from the events of everyday life. Many people who have had such an extraordinary experience are reluctant to give an account of the event to others because they fear they will be considered crazy. The lack of large numbers of accounts from Europe is inherently due to the skeptical attitude of the medical personnel there. In contrast to the USA, where hospital personnel are familiar with near-death experiences, little systematic research in the clinical field has been carried out in the "Old World."

Lurid films and strange research with the psychomanteum

A possible reason for this reluctance may be the fact that near-death experience is often treated as an esoteric phenomenon. Popular films such as *Ghost*, featuring Demi Moore and Patrick Swayze, may have contributed to many scientists regarding accounts of such experiences as frivolous.

But investigators of this phenomenon are also responsible to a large degree for the negative image of near-death research. For example, Elisabeth Kübler-Ross, who was previously well-known in the field of thanatology (the study of death and dying) for her conversations with the dying, has departed from her original work and now addresses esoteric themes. Raymond Moody, regarded as the groundbreaking pioneer of near-death research, has also applied himself to projects that generate little understanding among serious scientists. His attempts to establish contact with the dead with the help of mirrors in a so-called psychomanteum has drawn much criticism from his colleagues.

A psychomanteum is a room with a large mirror on the wall, which induces a so-called "hypnagogic state," i.e. a state of altered consciousness, in which visions, conversations with the dead, etc. are supposed to be possible.

We can only speculate about whatever may await us after death. Films such as *Flatliners* readily seize upon this theme. In *Ghost*, for example, a dead man attempts to communicate with his beloved wife.

The religious background of near-death experiences

Many accounts of experiences reflect the concept of the hereafter of a specific system of beliefs. Christians sometimes encounter Christ, Hindus their own gods, and Mormons are perhaps surprised to find that the strict hierarchical order of their religion also applies in the afterlife.

Most descriptions refer to a kind of tunnel, mist, or door at the beginning of the "journey." For some, this tunnel seems to be alive, as if it were an organism. Others see a bright, warm light at the end of the tunnel. What most people see is similar: it is associated with pleasant optical and acoustic impressions and appears as a preliminary stage on the journey to a paradisiacal hereafter.

Most people on the threshold to death mention early on being in a tunnel, a mist, or some kind of doorway, which they approach without fear.

One argument for the possible authenticity of near-death experiences is provided by paralyzed or blind people. How are they able to describe rooms they've never seen, or what was said during their operation?

Encounters with strange beings

Many accounts report an encounter with other people or beings. These are most often relatives or other loved ones who have already died: "most of all there was my girlfriend ... as well as my paternal grandmother. What really amazed me, in retrospect, was that I had never actually known her, because she died before I was born ... The greeting from these figures was overwhelming, it was basically a sea of love." (25)

As far as the place itself is concerned, people who have had near-death experiences tell us the following: "I entered a garden that dazzled with wonderful colors, which I cannot describe. They were like pastel colors, although this description isn't completely right." (25)

The architecture of the hereafter is also awesome in its form: bridges, libraries, and temples excel almost everything that is known on Earth. Often people mention having seen entire cities. But not all accounts describe concrete objects; some remain more vague and only describe an endless vastness or a beautiful expanse of light.

The problem of body and soul

Near-death experiences reflect an old understanding of humanity, namely, that body and soul are two separate entities. During near-death experience, the soul leaves the body, and in doing so takes the individual's personal identity with it. That part of an individual that makes us human, our ego, therefore exists independently of the physical body. This places near-death experience in an old philosophical and theological tradition based on the ability of the soul to separate itself from the body. This assumption has always been a part of esotericism, albeit in a more wide-ranging form. According to esoteric belief, an ethereal body also exists, in addition to the physical and the astral bodies. This ethereal body is responsible for sustaining the functions of life. The ancient supposition that physis and psyche—body and soul—are two separate entities is given new life by such reports.

Especially interesting are cases in which extra-corporeal awareness is documented. Sometimes ostensibly dead people have made observations that were impossible, either from their perspective or due to their physical condition. This is even more remarkable when the "apparently dead" person is lying in one room, but is aware of a completely different room, another floor, or even a building unknown to them. In a few cases, the person experiencing near-death was actually blind. What is more, paraplegics and leg amputees have apparently been able to move from where they were located. They have described rooms and people they could never have seen. In any event, the theme of body-and-soul, known since antiquity, will have to be considered anew in the light of near-death experiences.

According to their religion, Hindus encounter their gods; Christians see Mary or Jesus. A Christian recalls, "I really do mean Jesus Christ. There was no need or desire to worship him or to fall to my knees."

Beings of light and a mellow light

Many accounts of near-death include encounters with a being of light. According to most descriptions, this angel-like being is surrounded by a mellow, bright, but not blinding light. People feel utterly comfortable in this light. For them it means absolute happiness, all-embracing knowledge, and love for others and themselves. This light can be trusted implicitly without fear of loss; it eliminates all antagonism, and culminates in a feeling of deep bliss mingled with joy. In many cases, the presence of this light is interpreted religiously: "The next thing I can remember was that Jesus appeared to me. I really do mean Jesus Christ! There was no need or desire to worship him or to fall to my knees." (25)

Near-death experiences are regarded positively by many Catholic theologians. However, the Vatican does not consider them proof of either life after death nor the existence of God.

The churches and near-death experience

The German theologian Hans Küng soberly notes in his book *Eternal Life?* that no one who recounts a near-death experience has ever actually crossed the threshold of biological death. "Although on the threshold to death, they still have not crossed it. So what can such experiences of death tell us? Nothing! Such experiences of dying prove nothing about life after death." (26)

Many Catholic theologians regard near-death experiences positively. Episcopal letters reveal that although near-death experiences can be regarded as authentic, they cannot be considered insights into the hereafter or proof of God's existence. One representative of the Catholic Church recommended interpreting them not as proof, but as an indication of human transcendence; there were no known official Church misgivings. This is perhaps to be understood in the sense that if near-death experiences bring peace and joy, the possibility exists that they really are spiritual in nature.

Biblical characters in the West, Hindu gods in the East

Reactions from Protestant circles tend to be somewhat more skeptical. Here, too, it is emphasized that no one recounting the experience has truly died, making it impossible to make conclusive assertions about the hereafter. On no account can the Christian image of God be founded on near-death experiences.

Descriptions of the "beings of light" often associate them with biblical characters. Other observations and different interpretations can be found in a series of investigated accounts from other countries.

These differing reports support the supposition that the socio-cultural background of the person experiencing a state of near-death is decisive for the observations he or she makes. This applies both to awareness of exterior surroundings—primarily the architecture and clothing seen in the afterlife—as well as to the interpretation of the "being of light," which itself, interestingly, depends on the religious background of the person having the experience.

Investigation of experiences of near-death in India, for example, has revealed that mainly religious figures appear in that region, while reports from China are simply of a messenger, who is not further described, prompting immediate return.

A lifetime passes in review

A review of the individual's life is an often described occurrence. One report of the experience tells how the review consisted of countless pictures portraying scenes from that person's life.

Each scene was complete in itself. The invisible director had composed the whole review in such a way that the individual saw his death as the first scene and his birth as the last. Everything passed by at an amazing speed; he experienced his whole existence in rewind, so to speak, which left a deep impression on him.

Moral assessment and return

In some cases, the memory of the life they have lived so far is accompanied by a moral assessment of the events portrayed. It often includes the feelings of the people whom they affect: "At the same time, I felt the repercussions of all my deeds for all people … for air, earth, water, and plants." (25)

Someone else reported that "my conscience immediately assessed my deeds and judged me; that is to say, whether this or that deed was good or bad." (25)

The individual's return to their accustomed life takes place in various ways. In several cases, the encountered being of light is either present at the moment of return or in some way responsible for it. "The being told me that I had a mission, and that I had not yet begun this mission on Earth." (25)

Return to familiar, earthly life is often experienced as something painful. Sometimes the person near death would like to refuse to do so, but in all known cases this is of no avail.

A field of research with promise for the future

Near-death experience provides a fascinating field of research with great scope for further investigation. Everyone who has experienced near-death has radically changed their lives afterwards. Acquiring material goods has slipped into the background, making way for a more spiritually oriented lifestyle. Death has lost its fright. The modern-day starting point for explaining near-death experience is that a consciousness normally docked to the brain, which can be regarded as an information folder, is capable of temporarily separating from the body and, remaining active, gathers and absorbs information that it records in its non-corporeal "aggregate state."

The Hindu god Vishnu is one of the beings a Hindu may encounter during a near-death experience. Accounts often tell of a being who doesn't want the person to die because they still have a mission to fulfill.

SPIRITISM AND PARAPSYCHOLOGY

Approach and modus operandi

The initial goal of spiritism, inspired by researchers such as Swedenborg, was to prove the existence of an immortal soul independent of the material body. It assumes that an individual's personality continues to exist after death. Therefore, the possibility of making contact with the dead in the hereafter exists for those with the gift of being a medium.

Parapsychology currently deals with those phenomena that, from a scienctific point of view, belong more to the nebulous borderline areas of human thought and experience. Nevertheless, modern parapsychology initially has very little to do with spiritism. It has set itself the goal of painstakingly investigating, by means of scientific methods, all that spiritism believes to have discovered long ago and regards as certain scientific fact. But scientific investigation takes time, and parapsychology intends to provide hard evidence, no matter how difficult that may be. Phenomena such as those described below are currently being investigated and evaluated by parapsychologists.

In search of an operative scientific model

Much has changed in the public's perception of parapsychology and spiritism. The mediums, or sensitives, who are the main sources of information for spiritism, are no longer regarded as hysterics or mentally ill; telepathy (mind reading) and telekinesis (moving objects without the application of external force) are no longer considered deception and trickery, but scientific fact.

Instead, people with these gifts are taken seriously, as are other extraordinary phenomena. The task of parapsychology is to continue where previous spiritist researchers gave up, and to find a plausible model to adequately explain all these fringe phenomena. Specters, for example, belong to this field of investigation.

Faces from nowhere— a Spanish apparition

Maria Gomez Pereira of Bélmez, Spain was unable to forget August 23, 1971. On that otherwise perfectly unremarkable day, around midday, the eerie events that were to follow her for the rest of her life began.

Mrs. Pereira was busy preparing lunch in the kitchen of her home when, out of nowhere, a clearly recognizable image of a face suddenly appeared on the kitchen floor. The outlines of a man's face could be clearly seen. Maria Pereira tried in vain to remove the face from the kitchen floor. The face "refused" to be wiped away. One witness even thought that the face's expression changed. A week went by, and Mrs. Pereira resorted to more drastic measures. She simply pasted over the kitchen floor, covering up the eerie grimace— unfortunately to no avail.

As if she had issued a challenge to the spook, additional faces of both men and women appeared on the kitchen floor. Soon thereafter, they started appearing throughout the house. It is not surprising

Allegedly, genuine photographs have been taken of ghosts in haunted houses. Parapsychology tries to investigate such phenomena. One theory is that material can record and store images like a tape recorder.

The faces that suddenly appeared in Bélmez, Spain, have remained a puzzle for investigators. To date, no one has been able to prove them a swindle. But what are they?

that this incredible story of grimaces and ghostly faces was soon the talk of Bélmez.

Media coverage and attempted explanations

The press and countless photographers came to see for themselves and speculate about the phenomenon. Numerous photographs documented the existence of the uncanny faces. The mayor of the town demanded that the floor be renewed, and that a section of it should be preserved for further investigation as evidence of the faces' appearance. A variety of attempts were made to get to the root of the problem with countless chemical analyses and even an x-ray examination—with no practical results.

Was this odd form of haunting really no more than an extremely well thought-out trick? To this day, there is no evidence whatsoever to indicate this was the case. All that could be proven was that neither damp nor mold had caused the faces. For this purpose, a film had been specially embedded in the new floor. The only result was that the faces continued to appear. To date, no one has found a plausible explanation for their existence.

A gruesome find

It was then suspected that something underneath the floor of the house could be triggering the images. When workmen excavated the floor they found human skeletons, but without their skulls. Further investigation finally showed that the family's home is situated on the remains of a thirteenth-century cemetery.

By that time, the people of the area and the scientists involved in the case were convinced that this phenomenon was genuine. The discovered human remains were laid to rest in the cemetery of Bélmez in the hope that this would put an end to the haunting.

Unfortunately, this proved to be a false hope. The faces persisted just as stubbornly as before, and all attempts to explain the haunting have failed. Microphones have recorded voices and strange sounds that have been interpreted as moans and groans—obviously the laments of people who have suffered greatly.

Maria Pereira died in 2004, at the age of 85. Since then, the spook has found a new home: the faces now appear in the house in which she was born, only a hundred yards away. To date, more than twenty of these faces have been documented in the second location.

A haunting is often associated with an unatoned murder—as if the victim has to return as a ghost to remind the living of his gruesome fate.

Latest research

So far, there is no tenable evidence for the existence of ghostly apparitions, but also no counterevidence in favor of a rational explanation of the cases known to us. Paranormal events such as poltergeists or knocking spirits have in many cases been traced back to a source with a specific person with serious psychological problems or an adolescent at its center. It has been discovered that they are at least the trigger for such mysterious phenomena, although the apparent supernatural occurrences themselves could not be explained. It seems there are still many psychological processes beyond our comprehension. Of course, many cases have proven to be the result of deception or imagination. But, as is so often the case, there remains a small residue of inexplicable and mysterious accounts.

Rupert Sheldrake's new approach

A new starting point could be provided by the theory of the British biochemist Rupert Sheldrake, according to which there exist so-called morphogenetic fields that are free of material and energy and yet effectual over time and space, providing an invisible connection between living beings. The existence of such a field could explain phenomena such as telepathy, telekinesis, and even spirit apparitions.

According to Sheldrake, such a morphogenetic field is not limited to the brain, but extends beyond the body into its surroundings. These fields, which are currently the subject of a great deal of attention in Russia, are also known as life fields because they encompass everything. We human beings are in resonance with them, all on the same level of reso-

Spiritist sessions were the social event of the nineteenth century. Most were based on clever manipulation. However, the small residue of speculation that remains provides material for serious research.

nance, on one frequency. According to Sheldrake, this resonance connects all of us to the collective memory of our society and culture, and ultimately the collective memory of all mankind.

Another attempt at explanation

The physical phenomena of spiritism, which include events such as telekinesis, table-turning, and materializations (the visible manifestation of spirits), have in themselves ultimately failed to provide proof of life after death.

Knocking spirits are no proof of a hereafter. From an animist viewpoint, they can be thoroughly and completely explained by the concept that not only all living beings have souls, but also objects.

A spook in 2006

An eerie incident was reported in Deltona, Florida at the beginning of 2006. The spooky phenomena there even fascinated a film team. At the Dunnam household, objects had clearly been moving about without human involvement. Even sounds and voices from other dimensions could be heard and a terrifying ghostly apparition had provided material for a film team: the owners of the house—Edd and Beth Dunnam—were almost brought to desperation when a headless man appeared standing at the bedside of their two sons. Everything had begun quite harmlessly with a few "cold spots in the house," the Dunnams reported (27).

Spook stories from Ireland

Nerve-racking spooks don't only take place in Britain, Spain, and the USA, they can also be found on the Emerald Isle, Ireland. Here, countless houses have been infamous for centuries for frightening black cats that appear at night, for shadowy figures flitting through dimly-lit corridors, and long-dead noble ladies who terrify the living by silently gliding down stately staircases at midnight. Creepy things are told, for example, about Iveagh House on St. Stephen's Green in Dublin, the present-day seat of the foreign ministry. Every Maundy Thursday a mysterious cross allegedly appears in a specific window, the exact scene of the murder of the Archbishop of Cashel in 1583. A little girl called Mary Masters is said to haunt the prestigious Shelbourne Hotel, where she is supposed to have met a gruesome death. Parapsychologists explain that sometimes strong electromagnetic fields can cause fear in people and trigger off certain images. In addition, special architectural features, such as high ceilings, dark passageways, diffuse lighting conditions, and old walls are all conducive to experiencing ghostly phenomena. This can explain away much, but by no means everything.

Famous sites like the Shelbourne Hotel in Dublin attract people who want to experience something creepy. Some are disappointed, while others insist they have experienced something. Is it all imagination?

OUTLOOK

Throughout the ages, people have concerned themselves with life after death. Until the last few decades, science has mostly steered clear of this subject; however, things are slowly changing in the twenty-first century.

Quantum physics and modern-day cosmology have presented new, sensational models of how the universe and life itself came into existence. These theories are also relevant for the question of life after death. The beginnings of research in the field of near-death experiences and other paranormal phenomena demonstrate that many researchers are willing to acknowledge the possibility of a consciousness outside of, or apart from, the body. These incredible aspects are currently the subject of more detailed investigation.

Seth, who contacted the gifted medium Jane Roberts from the hereafter, described himself as a personality energy core no longer centered in physical form. Several researchers, including the physicists Burkhard Heim, Illobrand von Ludwiger, or Professor Ernst Senkowski, suspect that consciousness is matter of the highest frequency from a higher dimension.

If this is so, the individual therefore extends into other dimensions, including the afterlife. This new perspective allows the human body and death to be considered from a scientific point of view in a new and different way. Religion and esoterics have always known this, as has been shown.

All that remains is for this knowledge to be confirmed scientifically.

An encounter with a spirit can be portrayed like this, a nebulous shape that dissolves when you reach out to touch it. But spirits are sometimes described as real figures that appear like normal people.

Children also "appear" to the living, at least according to reports. Spiritists explain that they have often died in accidents and haunt the site where it happened, thinking they are still alive.

SOURCES

1   Herodotus. *The Histories*. Trans. Aubery de Selincourt. New York and London: Penguin Classics, 2003.

2   Budge, E. A. Wallis, ed. *The Egyptian Book of the Dead*. Kessinger Publications, 2005.

3   Giebel, Marion. *Das Geheimnis der Mysterien*. Munich: Patmos Verlag, 1990.

4   Homer. *The Odyssey*. Trans. Allen Mandelbaum. Bantam Classics, 1991.

5   Klimkeit, Hans-Joachim, ed. *Tod und Jenseits im Glauben der Völker*. Wiesbaden: Harrassowitz, 1978.

6   Guyonvarch, Christian-J. and Le Roux, Francoise. *Die Druiden*. Arun Verlag, 1995.

7   Simek, Rudolf. *Dictionary of Northern Mythology*. Trans. Angela Hall. D.S. Brewer, New Ed edition, 2006.

8   Isaiah 14:10–11, Revised Standard Version.

9   Alighieri, Dante: *The Divine Comedy*. Trans. John Ciardi. New York: Penguin Books, New American Library, 2003.

10   www.Himmelsboten.de

11   Zürrer, Ronald. *Reinkarnation. Einführung in die Wissenschaft der Seelenwanderung*. Zurich: Jestetten, 2005.

12   Braun, Hans-Jürg. *Das Leben nach dem Tod*. Zurich, 1996.

13   Iqbal, Mohammad. *Botschaften des Ostens*. Stuttgart: Edition Erdmann, 1984.

14   Hawley, Jack, trans. *The Bhagavad Gita*. California: New World Library, 2001.

15   Kölver, Bernhard. *Das Weltbild der Hindus*. Reimer: Berlin, 2003.

16   Ulrich, Hans R. *Von Meister Eckhardt bis Carlos Castaneda*. Frankfurt: Fischer Taschenbuchverlag, 1986.

17   Kant, Immanuel. *Träume eines Geistersehers, erläutert durch Träume der Metaphysik*. Ditzingen, 1976.

18   Hentschel-Heinegg, Aglaja. *Kontakte mit Unsichtbaren*. Frankfurt: Fischer Taschenbuchverlag, 1980.

19   Kerner, Justinus. *Die Seherin von Prevorst*. Stuttgart: Steinkopf, 1991.

20   Von der Leyen, Eugenie. *Meine Gespräche mit armen Seelen*. Aschaffenburg: Christiana Verlag, 1980.

21   Roberts, Jane. *Seth Speaks*. Amber-Allen, 1994 (reprint).

22   Van Praagh, James. *Reaching to Heaven*. London: Spiritual Horizons, 1999.

23   Browne, Silvia. *The Other Side and Back*. New York: Penguin Putnam, New American Library, 2002.

24   Moody, Raymond, M.D. *Life After Life*. Bantam, 1979.

25   Högl, Stefan. *Nahtoderfahrungen und Jenseitsreisen*. Marburg, 2000.

26   Küng, Hans: *Eternal Life?* Herder and Herder, 1991.

27   www.Paranews.net

Dietzelbinger, Konrad. *Mysterienschulen*. Munich, 1997.
Dunne, John J. *A Ghostwatcher's Guide to Ireland*. Pelican, 2001.
Ford, Arthur. *The Life Beyond Death*. Putnam's Sons, 1971.
Hornung, Eric. *Das geheime Wissen der Ägypter*. Munich, 2003.
Koran. New York: Penguin Classics, 7th ed., 2000.
Lucadou, Walter. *Dimension PSI*. Berlin, 2003.
Meckelburg, Ernst. *Jenseits der Ewigkeit*. Munich, 2000.
Murphet, Howard. *Beyond Death*. Theosophical Publishing, 1990.
Roberts, Marc. *Das Neue Lexikon der Esoterik*. Munich, 1995.

PICTURE CREDITS

INDEX